Lightning Death

Patrick Stephens Limited, a member of the Haynes Publishing Group, has published authoritative, quality books for enthusiasts for more than twenty years. During that time the company has established a reputation as one of the world's leading publishers of books on aviation, maritime, military, model-making, motor cycling, motoring, motor racing, railway and railway modelling subjects.
Readers or authors with suggestions for books they would like to see published are invited to write to: The Editorial Director, Patrick Stephens Limited, Sparkford, Nr. Yeovil, Somerset BA22 7JJ.

Lightning Death

The story of the Waffen-SS

Bruce Quarrie

Patrick Stephens Limited

First published in 1991

British Library Cataloguing in Publication Data
Lightning Death
Quarrie, Bruce 1947–
The Waffen-SS
1. Germany. Waffenschutzstaffel, history
I. Title
355.00943

ISBN 1–85260–075–6

Patrick Stephens Limited is a member of the Haynes Publishing Group P.L.C., Sparkford, Nr Yeovil, Somerset BA22 7JJ

Typeset by Burns & Smith Ltd

Printed in Great Britain

2 4 6 8 10 9 7 5 3 1

Contents

Introduction

Why, you might well ask, *another* book on the Waffen-SS? It would be a fair question, and the short answer is that this one is intended as a guide, especially to help anyone coming fresh to the subject to sort through the vast amount of much more detailed information (and misinformation) already available; it aims to show why and how the Waffen-SS ('Weapon-SS') evolved from a tiny personal bodyguard for one man into a multi-racial army of nearly a million men, and to provide pointers for more in depth research for those who want to learn more. For that reason, much information subsidiary to the main theme is given in the form of footnotes so as not to interrupt the narrative. A degree of simplification has been inevitable because the origins of the Waffen-SS and their relationship both to other branches of Himmler's odious organization and to the remainder of the German armed forces is extremely complex, for Nazi Germany was first and foremost a bureaucracy founded upon paperwork and political intrigue.

One of the most difficult tasks a writer faces is judging how much information a reader wants. How much does he or she already know? Here I have taken a middle course, presupposing a basic knowledge of the principal events of the Second World War but little knowledge of the Waffen-SS other than the usual assumption that it was responsible for all the atrocities. To get the latter out of the way first — it was not. Soviet Russian war crimes and 'crimes against humanity' before, during and after the 1939–45 period far exceed all those committed by the Nazis; and the western Allies, while less culpable, must bear their own burden of shame, as discussed later.

The Waffen-SS was a unique military organization. From its insignificant beginnings, after 1929 it grew in the hands of Heinrich Himmler into a sort

Left *SS PzKpfw V Panther tanks during the 'Battle of the Bulge' in December 1944. Panthers rarely carried any identifying unit insignia.*

of private empire within the new German empire or *Reich*. Uniformed like regular German Army soldiers but with their own organization, ranking system, high command, judiciary, commissariat and an oath avowing sole loyalty and honour to their Führer, the men of the Waffen-SS's premier units were among the finest fighting soldiers the world has ever seen, whatever their other faults, and herein lies the seemingly endless fascination with them.

It is now 50 years since the title 'Waffen-SS' became official but its very mention is still extremely emotive and I have therefore been careful to be as dispassionate as possible and to leave value judgements to the reader. To sum them up as either a bunch of thugs or as crusaders in a European war against Communism would be equally simplistic, although they have been portrayed as both. Their ranks included idealists as well as pragmatists, the chivalrous as well as the sadistic. For the most part they fought hard and effectively, spearheading many of the German Army's most successful offensives and being used as a 'fire brigade' to plug gaps in the line when other formations around them were crumbling. If this book leads to a greater understanding it will have achieved its purpose.

Bruce Quarrie
Wellingborough

1

Origins

In order to understand the Waffen-SS — both what it was and equally what it was not — it is necessary to understand something of its background, the framework so to speak, within which it existed. This means a short political history lesson, for which I apologize. Readers already familiar with German politics in the 1920s and '30s and with the infrastructure of the Nazi state may wish to skip the next few pages.

The SS — the initials stand for *SchutzStaffel* or 'protection squad' — was one of six German organizations whose members were all jointly put on trial for 'crimes against humanity' at Nürnberg (Nuremberg) after the Second World War. The others were the Nazi Party leadership, the Reich (Empire) Cabinet, the SA (*SturmAbteilung* or 'assault unit', popularly known as the 'Brownshirts'), the OKW (*OberKommando der Wehrmacht* or armed forces high command) and the Gestapo (an acronym for *Geheime StaatsPolizei*, secret state police). The fact that the Gestapo was indicted separately from the SS often surprises people who assume from films and popular fiction that they were one and the same. In a sense they were, and this is just one of many technicalities in the complex interlocking of the Third Reich's administrative and executive bureaucracy. In some ways they are all inextricable, as one man *could* have been a member of all six organizations. Some degree of simplification is therefore unavoidable in the following paragraphs, for which I hope readers will forgive me.

First, the Nazi Party. The *NationalSozialistische Deutsche ArbeiterPartei* (NSDAP) or National Socialist German Workers' Party was formed in München (Munich) in 1919 by a railway locksmith, Anton Drexler, as just the DAP (German Workers' Party). Its name was changed in April the following year, seven months after the former Army Corporal and Iron Cross winner, Adolf Hitler, joined it as, coincidentally, committee member number seven. At the time it was merely one of dozens of 'lunatic fringe' organizations which abounded in Germany in the aftermath of the First World War, since everybody had their own ideas about who was

Corporal Adolf Hitler, seated on the right, served in the dangerous role of a message runner with the 16th Bavarian Infantry Regiment throughout the First World War, being awarded the Iron Cross First Class in April 1918.

responsible for the country's defeat and the humiliating terms of the Treaty of Versailles signed in June 1919, and had their own remedies for Germany's political and and economic problems. Ironically, Hitler himself was originally assigned by the Army to investigate the new Party as part of a general check on 'subversive' movements in Germany! He found its aims to his liking, and his own mesmerising demagoguery rapidly led to his becoming its leader just over a year after he obtained his Army discharge in April 1920.

Hitler's own biography is so well known that there is no point in repeating it here, apart from remarking that it seems to have been from fellow soldiers returned from the Eastern Front that he developed his pronounced anti-Communist views; no one can actually answer for his anti-Semitism, but it may have originally stemmed from the fact that the doctor attending his mother at the time of her death in 1907 was Jewish.

Many early Nazi Party members were in the *Freikorps* ('Volunteer Corps'), a loose 'coalition', for want of a better word, of disenchanted ex-front line soldiers whose principal motivation was their being anti-Communist. Like a large number of other people, they felt that the armed forces had been betrayed by the war profiteers and draft dodgers — who were, of course, either Communists or Jews, or both... These men formed the cadre of the SA whose original function was to keep order at Party meetings. It was from a Freikorps unit, the Ehrhardt Brigade, that the Nazis adopted the Swastika as their emblem, while the Nazi Party salute was itself inherited from the Freikorps, whom Hitler professed to admire greatly. The *Totenkopf* or death's head emblem, which later became almost synonymous with the SS, was also adopted from Freikorps units of Baltic extraction.

The SA itself was formed in München in 1921 by one of Hitler's chauffeurs and bodyguards, Emil Maurice, and was subsequently led by an Army Captain called Ernst Röhm. It acquired its nickname from its uniform, a consignment of brown shirts originally intended for troops in East Africa. In 1923 a small squad of SA men were equipped with black ski caps as well, and led by Hitler's other chauffeur/bodyguard, Julius Schreck, a veteran of the Erhardt Brigade, they were given the task of protecting Hitler himself. They were known as the *Stosstruppe Hitler* (Shock Troop Hitler): the SS title lay some two years in the future and did not become official until 9 November 1925. But this is getting ahead of the story.

The use of the word 'Socialist' in the Nazi Party's title is as misleading as 'Workers' because both suggest a left-wing movement in which the

Members of the Freikorps in Berlin during March 1919 with an Erhardt armoured car bearing the death's head symbol which would later be adopted by the SS.

'workers' (which in those days meant mainly manual labourers and artisans) would control their country's destiny, and this, of course, was also the manifesto of the Communists, the Nazis' most bitter rivals for power. Nevertheless, the Party programme had a wide appeal to the working classes, particularly in rural areas, and by 1930 some 40 per cent of its members were categorized as farmers and 'workers'. The key words in the Party name, however, are actually 'National' and 'German', for it was first and foremost a patriotic movement.

The initial two clauses in the Party's 25-point manifesto stressed the need for the unification of all German peoples in a 'Greater Germany', and rejection of the Treaty of Versailles. It was in some ways an idealistic document which went on to declare that the state's first duty was to the livelihood of its citizens and that all citizens should have equal rights and responsibilities within the state; that jobs should be acquired by merit rather than through favouritism; that large businesses should be nationalized and that workers should share in profits; and that the state should encourage and help small businesses. It also called for land reforms, improvements in the educational system and in maternity benefits, tougher penalties for criminals, and carried a guarantee of religious freedom — with one specific exclusion: no Jew was to be allowed German citizenship. Other ominous clauses declared the German people's right to *Lebensraum* ('living room') in which the population could expand to fulfil its 'God-given destiny'; that non-citizens should be ineligible for state benefits; and called for a halt to all non-German immigration.

In the chaos in Germany during the immediate post-war era, the rallying

The first four SA standards being presented in München in 1923.

Julius Schreck, centre, with members of the original Stosstruppe Hitler *wearing brown SA uniforms with swastika armbands and black ski caps. From this tiny beginning the Waffen-SS would grow to an army of 910,000 men.*

cries of 'Germany for the Germans' and 'law and order' were particularly attractive to a large number of people, although the Nazi Party's growth was still slow to begin with. Nor was the movement's avowed anti-Semitism as repulsive to most people then as it would be now — and neither was the feeling confined to Germany alone. Many Englishmen and Americans, Italians, Frenchmen and Russians, were as ill-disposed towards the Jews as were similar numbers of Germans of the time. It is only the horror of the Holocaust, as the Nazi persecution of the Jews has come to be called, which has introduced guilt feelings in the majority of people and brought a virtual halt to anti-Semitism in most countries. Those people who still share the old feelings are largely too shamefaced by what their peers would think to express them. Racialism was, and is, not the exclusive prerogative of the Nazis. Supposedly Communist Russia's slate is hardly clean in this respect! What the Nazi Party's anti-Semitism actually did was to provide a focus for the resentment thousands of people felt for their country's impoverished state, a resentment which would increase with galloping inflation* and unemployment.

* In 1918 there were 19 Marks to the pound Sterling (or four Marks to the American dollar); by November 1923, at the time of the attempted putsch, the rate was 604,500 *million* to one (or 130,000 million to the dollar)! A wheelbarrow was, literally, more valuable than all the banknotes it could carry.

By as early as 1923 the Nazi Party had 70,000 members and, inspired by Benito Mussolini's Blackshirts' successful *coup d'état* in Italy the previous year, Hitler attempted a similar putsch to take over the state government of Bavaria. He was supported in this by the popular and heroic First World War Chief-of-Staff, General Erich Ludendorff. The choice of Bavaria as the Nazi Party's base was not accidental. Despite the unification of Germany by Bismarck in the 1860s, Bavaria had retained a great deal of internal autonomy, and during the First World War provided three Army Korps numbered separately from the regular Imperial forces. Bavaria had its own War Ministry and promotion system as well. In the immediate post-war period this gave rise to strong pro-Austrian separatist feelings and a sense that the popular Kronprinz (Crown Prince) Rupprecht had been betrayed by the Prussians. This in turn resulted in a right-wing state government which was frequently at loggerheads with Berlin.

Seeking to exploit these differences, on 8 November 1923 some 600 SA men surrounded the Bürgerbräukeller in München where the State Commissioner, Gustav Kahr, was giving a speech. Hitler, accompanied by the former fighter ace Hermann Göring and other leading Nazis, burst into the crowded beer hall and fired a pistol at the ceiling to command attention. Kahr and his immediate associates were hustled into a back room and forced to agree to co-operate with the Nazis' plans, but the following day, free from intimidation, they called out the Army and police to disperse a Nazi rally in the city centre. Shots were fired, several people were killed and both Hitler and Göring were wounded. Göring succeeded in fleeing, eventually ending up in Sweden, but Hitler was arrested and in February 1924 was tried for high treason. Considering the offence, the five-year jail sentence he received was mild, but the Nazi Party and the SA were both declared illegal organizations and forced underground. Somehow the fledgling SS organization was ignored in these bans. Röhm was not imprisoned but *was* cashiered from the Army. Ludendorff, to his personal indignation, was found not guilty and discharged, to cheers from the spectators.

Hitler's incarceration in Landsberg prison was brief, and he was released in December of the same year after agreeing that in future he would only work within the constitution. 'If out-voting them takes longer than out-shooting them,' he declared cynically, 'at least the results will be guaranteed by their own constitution.' But imprisonment was a cathartic experience for him and it was during those 10 months that he began dictating his political testament, *Mein Kampf* ('My Struggle'), to his secretaries, Emil Maurice and, later, Rudolf Hess.

During Hitler's imprisonment, one of his anti-Semitic colleagues, Alfred Rosenberg, formed a new Party under a different name, aided by the influential politician Gregor Strasser; similarly, Röhm kept the SA more or less intact under different guises such as sports clubs and similar organizations. The boisterous behaviour, the drinking, singing, swearing and fighting that characterized the SA from the outset did little to help the

Party's image, as Hitler was early to discover! Both of the bans proved to be only short-term measures though, and two months after Hitler's release from prison the new 'Freedom Party' was dissolved and the Nazi party re-established at a well-attended meeting in the Bürgerbräukeller. From this point there was no looking back, although there were problems.

First, Hitler quarrelled with Röhm, who wanted to make the SA independent of the Party. Even this early, Hitler saw that the SA, who considered themselves a 'people's army' and were already viewed with suspicion by the regular Army, could pose a threat to his own power. He therefore refused Röhm's demands. The portly homosexual resigned and later went out to Bolivia with a military mission, leadership of the SA being taken over by Captain Pfeffer von Salomon. In the meantime, while Hitler's following was still in Bavaria, in the north of Germany, Gregor Strasser established himself as a clear rival for the Party leadership.

Strasser's views differed quite widely from Hitler's: in particular they were not so overtly anti-Semitic or anti-Communist, and in fact, he called for an alliance with Soviet Russia against the 'imperialist' powers, Britain and France. His ideas were also more genuinely 'socialist' and included a scheme for farm collectives, and his views were supported by an energetic and influential young journalist called Josef Göbbels. This situation soon became intolerable to Hitler and in February 1926 he called a Party meeting in Bamberg during which his oratory defeated Strasser, discredited his ideas and won Göbbels over to the Hitlerite Party line.

With his supremacy now assured, Hitler moved from strength to strength, one of his staunchest supporters being a mild-mannered, be-spectacled agricultural chemistry student turned poultry farmer called Heinrich Himmler. Another veteran of the beer hall putsch, Himmler had also supported Strasser to begin with but on changing his allegiance was rewarded with deputy leadership of the SS. At this time the commander of the *SchutzStaffel* was Josef Berchtold, then also editor of the Nazi Party newspaper, the *Völkischer Beobachter* ('People's Observer'*). Their duties in the tiny SS — which only numbered 200 men organized in groups of about 20 in various German cities in 1926 — were hardly onerous and for the time being the principal task of the SS men was canvassing advertising for the paper! The situation would only really begin to change in 1929.

By that time Nazi Party membership had passed 100,000 and they had won 12 seats in the Reichstag, the Weimar Republic's parliament. Then, on 16 January 1929, Himmler was made Reichsführer ('empire leader') of the SS, which now numbered all of 280 men. It was still vastly out-numbered by the SA, who fielded 60,000 men at the Nürnberg Party rally that August, but under Himmler it would gradually acquire more and more power, first in secret then more openly until eventually the tentacles of the SS would reach into every layer of German society. Apart from the

---

* *Volk*, 'people', actually meant the *German* people, and the newspaper's editorial bias was unashamedly anti-Semitic.

The aging President Hindeburg takes the salute at a parade on 27 August 1933, shortly after the appointment of Hitler as Chancellor. Behind him are Hitler himself, trades union leader Dr Robert Ley and Hermann Göring.

Russian secret police it would become the most feared organization the world has ever seen, although no one could have predicted this in 1929.

The following year, 1930, was a decisive one in the Nazis' rise to power. Following the resignation of the last Social Democrat Chancellor, Hermann Müller, in March, the NSDAP approached the September Reichstag elections with confidence. With a paid-up membership approaching a quarter of a million, they succeeded in winning 107 seats in the Reichstag, making the NSDAP the country's second largest party: the Social Democrats were still in front with 143 seats and the Communists were third with 77. Moreover, the SA itself now actually outnumbered the tiny 100,000-man Army which was all Germany was allowed under the terms of the Treaty of Versailles. This strength was making the Army itself increasingly nervous, and when three Army officers were tried on charges of spreading Nazism, Hitler himself appeared before the tribunal to assure the Generals that the SA was not a rival to them. (Three years earlier, in 1927, the Army had banned members of the NSDAP from being recruited into its ranks.) In fact, Hitler was at great pains to press the point that without the backing of the Nazi Party, the Army itself would wither and become a Marxist tool.

The year 1931 also saw two significant developments. The aging President Hindenburg officially received Hitler for the first time, and Röhm was persuaded to return from his self-imposed exile to take over the SA once more. By March of 1932 the SA was 400,000 strong and fears that it might attempt a *coup d'état* caused it to be banned for the second time. Its members were rightly feared by many people because in addition to physically beating those who refused to contribute to Party funds, SA members frequently disrupted rival political meetings, particularly those of the Communists; and there were numerous street brawls resulting in several hundreds of deaths over the years.

However, this ban was also short-lived, for in the same year's elections the Nazis won 239 seats in the Reichstag, which due to the German system of proportional representation, made them the largest party even though they only had 37 per cent of the vote. The Catholic Centre Party politician, Franz von Papen, a former Army General Staff officer, succeeded Heinrich Brüning as Chancellor; a moderate, he hoped to be able to control the Nazis, but this dream proved futile. Meanwhile, Hermann Göring had been appointed Prussian Minister of the Interior, giving him command of the Prussian police force, while in March the following year Himmler became Police President of München, giving the Nazis control of the two most powerful law enforcement agencies in Germany. They also succeeded in merging the SA with the *Stahlhelm* ('steel helmet') organization of ex-servicemen, whose President was Hindenburg.

Even before this, the Nazis had set up two new unofficial offices which were to emerge as the most feared of all alongside the Gestapo, which was itself established in 1933 by Göring (who had been elected President of the Reichstag in July 1932). These were the SD (*SicherheitsDienst*), the Nazi security service whose leader was the brilliant, albeit cruel, cold and calculating ex-naval officer Reinhard Heydrich; and the RuSHA (*Rasse und SiedlungsHauptAmt*) or Race and Resettlement Office, under the agronomist, Walter Darré. (It was largely the latter's ideas on selective breeding which gave the inspiration for Himmler's mad 'Aryan' theories, discussed later.) RuSHA established the original standards for enlistment in the SS and checked the ancestry of potential brides for SS men. More ominously, it also dictated the resettlement policies designed to hand over properties and businesses to 'pure' Germans by evicting their original owners, many of whom would eventually end up in one of the concentration camps. Both the SD and RuSHA were integral parts of the SS with overall allegiance to Himmler.

Another significant development in March 1933 was the official formation of an armed SS bodyguard for Hitler, the *Leibstandarte 'Adolf Hitler'*, under Josef 'Sepp' Dietrich, an energetic though uneducated First World War soldier and Freikorps veteran. The LAH derived from the original *Stosstruppe* and had become the 120-strong guard of the Nazi Party headquarters in München, the *Braunehause* ('brown house'), in 1931, with the intermediate title *Stabwache* ('staff watch'). Its members were rigorously selected on the grounds of racial purity, height, and physical and moral fitness, having to be between the ages of 23 and 35 and without any vestige of a criminal record. It was to grow into one of the most formidable fighting formations at the disposal of the Third Reich, the premier unit in what would later become known as the Waffen-SS. Before this could happen, though, Hitler had to gain overall power in Germany.

In August 1932 Hindenburg had refused Hitler the Chancellorship, giving von Papen the post. Now the Minister of Defence, General Kurt von Schleicher, leapt into the breach and at the end of November persuaded

Reinhard Heydrich in Gruppenführer's uniform at the height of his power.

The Stabwache *in München in 1930. The SS uniform is becoming recognizable by this time. 'Sepp' Dietrich is third from left in the front row.*

Hindenburg that the Army had no confidence in von Papen. He tried to form a coalition with Gregor Strasser but Strasser and Hitler quarrelled again, and Strasser resigned. Schleicher's coalition government lasted all of 57 days. He was dismissed after proposing to dissolve the Reichstag, and Hindenburg appointed Hitler Chancellor in his place in January 1933, with von Papen as Vice-Chancellor. He had accomplished what he had promised in Landsberg — the achievement of power through constitutional means. However, this power was still far from being absolute.

The coalition with the Centre Party soon fell apart and Hitler called for fresh elections in March. Then, during the night of 27 February, the Reichstag was set on fire. The Communists were blamed and Göring's police, helped by the Berlin SS* and some 50,000 SA auxiliaries, rounded

* The Berlin SS was commanded by another former Freikorps man, Kurt Daluege, who would later become head of the *Ordnungspolizei* and succeed Heydrich as Protector of Bohemia and Moravia after the latter's assassination in May 1942. The *Ordnungspolizei* or 'order police' (usually abbreviated to 'Orpo') was one of four branches of the German police force, the others being the Gestapo, the *Kriminalpolizei* or 'criminal police' ('Kripo') and the

Curious Berliners gathered to look at the smouldering Reichstag on the morning of 28 February 1933.

up thousands of Communists and liberals under an emergency decree suspending civil liberties. This enabled the Nazis to increase their share of the vote to 44 per cent which, with the support of the smaller but similarly right-wing Nationalist Party under the wealthy industrialist Alfred Hugenberg, gave them a majority in the Reichstag. It was the Communist Party which was then banned, all of its Deputies ('MPs') losing their seats, and over the next three months pretexts were found for abolishing all the other parties, the Nationalists being the last to go when Hungenberg resigned on 14 July. For the next 12 years Germany would be a one party state, while Himmler's SS would grow to become in effect a state within the state.

Sicherheitspolizei or 'security police' ('Sipo'). To rationalize this complex situation, Himmler, who had been appointed Chief of the German Police (*Chef de Deutschen Polizei*) in 1936, ordered the creation of a new co-ordinating office. The *Reischs SicherheitsHauptAmt* (RSHA), or Main Office of Reich Security, was officially formed in September 1939. Run by Heydrich until his death and thence by the burly Austrian Ernst Kaltenbrunner, the RSHA administered the SD, Sipo, Kripo and Gestapo. It was the RSHA which also formed and controlled the extermination squads, the *Einsatzgruppen*, discussed on page 76.

2

Consolidation and expansion 1933-9

During 1933 the SS leapt in size to over 50,000 men while the SA, about 300,000 strong at the beginning of the year, grew to nearly three million by its end as previous waverers jumped on the Nazi Party bandwagon. These 'March Violets' were generally despised by the old comrades of the 1923 putsch who were entitled to wear the Blood Order, one of the highest of several political decorations for service to the Party which Hitler was to introduce. Blood, and the concept of heroic sacrifice, became essential parts of Nazi ideology, so the following is a brief look at some of the mythology which was so fundamental to the principles of the Nazi Party and to the SS in particular.

Rudolf Hess (left) looks on seemingly impassively while Hitler, Röhm and Göring seem to be engaged in a fair old argument with someone — possibly Strasser, for this is a Nazi Party gathering in the late 1920s or early '30s after the introduction of the Blutorden *or Blood Order to commemorate the attempted 'beer hall putsch'.*

SA parade in Berlin, 30 January 1933.

The first and most important ingredient in this mythology was race. Hitler, Himmler, Rosenberg, Darré and others were convinced through a mixture of personal prejudice and their readings in such works as the Compte de Gobineau's *Essay on the Inequality of the Human Race* and Houston Stewart Chamberlain's *The Foundation of the Nineteenth Century* that they belonged to a superior race — a master race. They called this race 'Aryan' after the writings of the philologist Friedrich Max Müller, who died in 1900 and who would have been horrified to see the Nazi perversion of his theories. These dealt purely with the development of Indo-European languages and Müller was at pains to point out they had no relevance to racial differences, a disclaimer which the Nazis conveniently chose to ignore. Rosenberg himself cobbled together many of these earlier ideas and prejudices in his own turgid book *The Myth of the Twentieth Century*, which was published in 1930, five years after the first volume of *Mein Kampf*, and which became the second Nazi 'bible'.

The 'Aryans', argued the Nazi 'philosophers' by various tortuous means, were essentially the German people, although they admitted that the people of other nationalities — such as those of German extraction living abroad, particularly in the Balkans and many Belgians, Britons, Dutchmen and Scandinavians — also 'qualified' if they could prove a pedigree 'untainted' by Jewish blood. To join the SS in the early days, candidates had to be able to trace unblemished 'Aryan' ancestry back to 1750, but these initial standards were soon eroded in the desperate search for simple manpower when Germany found itself at war with most of the rest of the world, especially after 1941. Moreover, in their continuing search for 'respectability', Hitler and Himmler allowed many honorary members into the *Allgemeine* ('general') SS, giving particular encouragement to wealthy industrialists and scions of the old aristocracy — not all of whom appreciated the distinction!

Heinrich Himmler, from whom many of the crazier elements of Nazi mythology emerged, was an equal believer in the 'master race' but his fantasies went even further. Apart from being a great admirer of the medieval Mongol warlord Genghis Khan, he developed his own theories about the Teutonic Knights and even earlier Germanic expansion eastwards from Europe. Perhaps it was these ideas which led to his eventual acceptance of Croatians, Indians and even Ukrainians and Tartars into the SS, which began by being the epitome of the Nazi 'Aryan' ideal and ended

Himmler addressing troops of the Leibstandarte Adolf Hitler *after the award on their own standard. The scene is actually Metz and the date 1940; the man carrying the flag is Obersturmführer Heinrich Springer.*

up as an amorphous conglomeration of a dozen or more nationalities and creeds.

Himmler, the pedantic son of a Bavarian schoolmaster, had been born in 1900 and brought up in the Roman Catholic faith, against which he later rebelled. Although he volunteered, he just avoided military service during the First World War because of his youth, but joined the Freikorps in 1919. Austere in his personal habits — he was always notoriously short of money — he was fascinated by the history of the early German peoples. Henry (or Heinrich) the Fowler, who became uncrowned Emperor of the Holy Roman Empire in AD 916, came to be something of an obsession, and Himmler seems to have believed that he was actually his spiritual reincarnation. Henry had driven back the Hungarians and Slavs as well as annexing Lorraine into the Empire, and Himmler saw the Germanic 'crusade' against Soviet Russia as a continuation of this work.

He imbued the SS with mystical attributes, delving into the meanings of ancient runes from which many Nazi insignia were derived. He even had a replica of a medieval castle built at Wewelsburg, near Paderborn in Westfalia, which contained a chamber with a round table, modelled after the Arthurian legends popularized in Germany by the music of Wagner. It was here that he gathered his closest SS companions, although he never really had any intimate friends and most of those invited appear to have attended his meetings in the spirit of humouring a mental invalid rather than through any shared belief in his Aryan mythology!

With such a mystical attitude to life, it will come as little surprise to learn that Himmler was also a firm believer in homeopathic and herbal medicines, nor that, under Hitler's influence, he became a vegetarian. He believed that SS men should thrive on porridge and mineral water, and in fact Germany's entire mineral water bottling and distribution industry was nationalized under the SS *WirtschaftsVerwaltungHauptAmt* (WVHA), or economic administration department!*

The odd thing is that although Himmler hated priests (but was totally pragmatic in his dealings with the Vatican), he also borrowed extensively from the Jesuits in the structuring and ritual of the SS. With their strict moral code the Jesuits had been the 'storm troopers' of the Counter-Reformation, and in fact some of their ideals, particularly those of loyalty and strict obedience, had in turn been adopted from the Japanese Samurai warrior caste. The Portuguese missionary Francis Xavier had been one of the earliest European settlers in Japan, back in 1549, and his admiration for the Japanese code of bushido was taken up and adopted by the Order, from

---

* The WVHA also came to control the concentration and labour camps and handled the distribution and sale of goods manufactured in them, as well as running quarries, cement, brick and lime works, ceramic, textiles, leather and furniture factories and a variety of other enterprises. After the July 1944 attempt on Hitler's life it was was also made responsible for the V1 and V2 missile programmes. Basically a slave labour enterprise, the WVHA was run by Oswald Pohl who opposed the extermination of the Jews, not through humanitarian reasons but because he needed the manpower. Pohl was nevertheless hanged in 1951.

whom Himmler later also copied it. So close, in fact, were some of the parallels between the Society of Jesus and Himmler's SS that Hitler called him 'my Ignatius Loyola', after the Society's founder.

The SS motto, engraved on the dagger which was itself part of the overall mystique, is the key to the SS mentality: *Mein Ehre heißt Treue*, 'Loyalty is my Honour'. What made the SS motto unusual was that the loyalty was to one person alone — Adolf Hitler — rather than to an abstract such as the state or the constitution. This is shown in the SS oath, which in the Waffen-SS was only taken after basic military training had been completed. Candidates were initially accepted into the SS at a ceremony on 9 November, the anniversary of the beer hall putsch, and took the oath the following 20 April, Hitler's birthday. They then received their ceremonial dagger in October. In its final form the oath ran as follows:

'I swear to thee Adolf Hitler
As Führer and Chancellor of the German Reich
Loyalty and bravery.
I vow to thee and to the superiors whom thou shalt appoint
Obedience unto death
So help me God.'

Something of the mistrust and distaste he felt for the SA seems apparent on Hitler's face at this NSDAP rally at Braunschweig in 1931. Röhm is on the Führer's left.

The 'Judas', Victor Lutze, wearing the insignia of Chief of Staff of the SA on his black Allgemeine-SS uniform after Röhm's murder. Lutze died in a car crash in May 1943 and was replaced by Wilhelm Schleppmann, the last leader of the SA.

Hitler did not officially adopt the title 'Führer' ('leader') until he suspended the Presidency following Hindenburg's death on 2 August 1934, at which time he also made himself commander-in-chief of the armed forces. Before this happened, though, on 30 June 1934 Hitler had made one more move to cement his own position further.

The general membership of the SA was, relatively speaking, more left–wing than the rest of the Nazi Party, and many people had favoured Strasser rather than Hitler. There was also a feeling among most SA personnel that the 'revolution' should be a continuous process, and they feared that Hitler was too favourably disposed towards the traditional power groups in Germany, namely the aristocracy and the industrial magnates. It was time, Hitler decided, to show where the real power in Germany lay, to remove the threat to stability posed by the stormtroopers, and to reassure the armed forces. He had by this time realized that the Army, not the intransigent SA, was the real key to maintaining that power. He was also aware that there was still a great deal of general distrust of the Nazi Party, and particularly a dislike of its strong–arm methods. The way to resolve both problems seemed simple: destroy the leadership of the SA and terrorize its membership into subservience, at the same time casting blame for all the excesses in the NSDAP's past on the Brownshirts.

Still Hitler dithered. Despite their disagreements, Röhm *was* one of his oldest and closest comrades. It was Victor Lutze, the SA leader in Hannover, who finally started the ball rolling. He reported to Hitler a speech in which Röhm claimed that the SA was the true army of National Socialism and that the regular Army should be relegated purely to a training role. This, in the eyes of both the Party and the Army, was nothing less than treason. Hitler ordered Röhm to give the entire SA a month's leave during July. Then the ever-devious Göbbels invented a story that the Berlin SA were to be called out on 29 June. Lists were quickly drawn up in great secrecy of the SA 'ringleaders' who should be arrested and executed. Himmler, Heydrich, Göring and others, including Lutze, all played a part in this, naming personal as well as political enemies. Hitler's long–standing adversary Gregor Strasser was one of the casualties, shot in a Gestapo cell. The former Chancellor, Kurt Schleicher, was another.

On 30 June the Leibstandarte *Adolf Hitler* was alerted, and SS units were put on standby in Berlin, München and other centres. Hitler flew with Lutze to München where they arrested the leading SA officers and ordered them under SS escort to Stadelsheim prison to await their fate. Hitler, with an armed Leibstandarte escort, then drove to Bad Weissee where Röhm and other senior SA men were staying in an hotel. The SS men burst into their rooms, discovering Röhm and others in bed with their boyfriends. They were dragged out and also sent to Stadelsheim. Röhm himself, as an ex-Army officer, was offered the traditional pistol but refused to accept it. A codeword was flashed to Berlin and elsewhere and the SS moved in throughout Germany, taking the SA leaders into custody and promptly executing them by firing squad. Röhm was shot in his cell, protesting his loyalty to the last.

Last of the summer wine? SA and SS standard-bearers at Nürnberg in 1934.

The Leibstandarte on parade in München on 9 November 1935. In the foreground is Theodor Wisch who would later command the division in Normandy in 1944. At the time of writing he is still alive, aged 82.

No certain figure for the total number of SA men murdered over 30 June/1 July 1934 has ever emerged. The minimum is 77, this being the figure Hitler announced to the Reichstag in a special address on 13 July, but more realistic estimates put it at between 400 and 1,000 and it may have been even higher. Whatever the true number, the result was the emasculation of the SA which, under its new leader, Lutze, ceased to be of any significance in German politics. What the 'night of the long knives' also achieved was the beginning of the ascendancy of the SS within the military and political arena and its final independence from the SA.

Almost from the beginning, the SS had been seen as a select body within the hierarchy, an elite embodying all the cardinal Nazi principles. Now it had proved its worth in blood, most powerful of the Nazi symbols. In the early days of the SS symbolism was particularly strong, although it was to wither when faced with the realities of the Eastern Front, when the crusade against Communism and Slavic 'subhumanity' dissolved into a simple struggle for survival. The Blood Order, or *Blutorden*, as we have seen, was one of the most prestigious decorations within the Party. The Blood Banner (*Blutfahne*) was another powerful symbol. This was the flag carried at the time of the 1923 putsch, stained with the blood of the 'martyrs' killed in München's Feldherrnhalle. The Röhm purge similarly became known as the Blood Purge, and those members of the SS who had taken part in the massacre achieved their own form of Nazi immortality.

Other symbols were of similar importance. The use of Nordic lightning runes — *Sigrunen*, signifying victory — for the SS collar insignia was an inspiration. The skull and crossbones of the death's head (*Totenkopf*) was nothing new of course, and was also worn by the black-garbed troops of the Army's new armoured (*Panzer*) formations which would shortly be brought into being. Although it had long been used as a uniform device among light cavalry regiments of many different nationalities, in the SS the death's head affirmed a special willingness to die for the cause. The mixture of old and novel symbols was intended to suggest the creation of a new order which was nevertheless firmly rooted in the Germanic past, and to a degree which seems almost incredible today succeeded in establishing a sense of German unification and purpose which had never existed before. Hitler, of course, was a master of pageantry and the massed ranks of the SA and SS at Party rallies, the music, the speeches, the rousing songs, the hundreds of fluttering red, white and black banners, as well as Hitler's own oratory, exerted a mesmeric appeal on a population accustomed to the grey government of the Weimar Republic.

One branch of the SS used the death's head device on its collar patches,

The SS Sigrunen on the collar patch and the Totenkopf cap badge are clear in this portrait of Sturmbannführer Sylvester Stadler who later commanded the 9th SS Panzer Division Hohenstaufen. This photograph was taken on the Kharkov front in March 1943.

Left *The Luitpold Arena in Nürnberg in 1934 with men of the Leibstandarte* Adolf Hitler *drawn up in the foreground. Heinrich Himmler is on the Führer's right for the salute, Victor Lutze on his left.*

Below *Theodor Eicke, first commandant of Dachau concentration camp and later commander of the 3rd SS Division* Totenkopf, *pictured here during the advance into Russia in 1941, was a brutal, uneducated thug whose men nevertheless idolized him.*

instead of the *Sigrunen*, as well as on its caps. This was the *Totenkopfverbände*, or death's head band, the first unit of which was formed at Dachau in 1933 under the former policeman Theodor Eicke. (It was, in fact, Eicke who shot Röhm.) The task of the *Totenkopf* units was to guard the concentration camps which began springing up all over Germany in 1933. Originally called 're-education camps', a title which was soon abandoned, these were hutted compounds into which opponents of the new Nazi state were herded. To begin with most of their inmates were Communists, but Jews soon began to follow, along with gypsies, homosexuals, petty criminals, trade unionists and dissenters of all types. As the net of those taken into custody was cast wider, the need for more camps grew and Dachau was followed in quick succession by Buchenwald and Sachsenhausen, then Belsen, Mauthausen and Theresienstadt. The number eventually grew to twenty main camps with 65 satellites, most of them in Poland.

The camps were not initially places where extermination was a deliberate policy. That did not come until the beginning of 1942, following a conference of senior government officials and SS officers at Wannsee chaired by Reinhard Heydrich. Among those involved were Heinrich Müller, the erstwhile Bavarian policeman who had been appointed head of

Himmler (centre) accompanied by Reinhard Heydrich (on his right) inspecting an SS guard at the Hradcany Palace in Prague after Heydrich had been appointed 'Protector' of Bohemia and Moravia.

the Gestapo, and the formerly inconspicuous SD man Adolf Eichmann.*
It was Eichmann who was the principal architect of the 'final solution';
Heydrich himself seems to have seen the death camps as a mere extension
of the existing slave labour programme administered by the WVHA. The
result in either case was the annihilation of some six million Jews and
uncounted numbers of Russians, Poles and other nationalities, including
racial Germans.

The *Totenkopfverbände* was the second SS unit to carry arms officially, and
had helped the Leibstandarte *Adolf Hitler* execute the SA personnel arrested
during the Röhm purge. The ambitious Eicke soon expanded the duties of
his men, creating five battalions (*Sturmbanne*) of *Totenkopf* troops named
Oberbayern, *Elbe*, *Sachsen*, *Ostfriedland* and *Brandenburg*, the latter
sometimes being misleadingly confused with the Army's elite *Brandenburg*
Regiment of commandos. In 1937 these battalions were reorganized into
three regiments, *Oberbayern*, *Brandenburg* and *Thüringen*, to which was
added a fourth, *Ostmark*, after the German annexation of Austria in 1938.
These troops eventually became the 3rd Waffen-SS Division *Totenkopf* with
Eicke as their commander after he handed over administration of the
concentration camps to Richard Glücks.†

The relationship between the Waffen-SS, or 'Weapon-SS', and the
concentration camps is one which seems to provoke continuous contro-
versy, although it is actually perfectly simple. Apologists for the Waffen-SS
usually claim that they were merely ordinary soldiers who knew nothing
about the extermination of the Jews. In many cases, especially among the
rank and file, this is quite probably true. At the same time it cannot be
denied that there was a constant interchange of personnel between the
fighting formations — and not just the *Totenkopf* Division — and the
concentration camp guards. Men no longer considered fit for front line
service because of wounds or ill health were regularly transferred to camp
guard duties, their place being taken by younger and fitter men from the
camps. But — and it is a big but — this exchange process was not restricted
to the SS formations alone. As the need for more and more men to replace
front line casualties grew, especially after 1942, wounded Army, Navy and
Air Force personnel were also shunted into concentration camp duties and
given 'honorary' SS status and Waffen-SS paybooks. The Waffen-SS was

---

* 'Gestapo' Müller disappeared at the end of the war and has never been traced. It is possible
that he escaped to South America but another theory is that he found sanctuary in Russia,
of all places, using his files to buy immunity and help the KGB to establish its extensive
intelligence network in West Germany. Eichmann escaped to Argentina using a Vatican
passport, but was tracked down by the Israelis and kidnapped in 1961. Taken back to Israel,
he was tried and hanged.

† Glücks also disappeared at the end of the war. Eicke himself proved an energetic and
capable field commander who displayed considerable personal courage. An indication of the
esteem which his men held for him is shown in the fact that when he was killed after his
'plane was shot down behind Russian lines in 1943, a party of volunteers laid on a raid to
recover his body.

Brigadeführer Paul Hausser was the man principally responsible for licking the fledgling Waffen-SS into shape. Later he became the first SS officer to command an entire army when he took over Seventh Army from Dollmann in Normandy (see later). In between he commanded the Verfüg-ungstruppen, Das Reich *and I SS Panzer Korps.*

not, therefore, alone in sharing responsibility for the Holocaust, a point which is often ignored.

* * *

Apart from the Leibstandarte *Adolf Hitler* and the *Totenkopf* units, a third armed branch of the SS was also growing during 1933–4. A number of SS 'political purpose' squads had already been established in various cities, and when Hitler repudiated the Treaty of Versailles on 16 March 1935 and reintroduced conscription, these formed the nucleus of a third military SS formation, the *Verfügungstruppe* or 'special disposal' troop, a broad term which originally included the Leibstandarte as well.

Even before this, two SS officer training schools had been established at Bad Tölz and Braunschweig (Brunswick), the latter commanded by a retired Army Lieutenant-General named Paul Hausser who had accepted the equivalent SS rank of Brigadeführer (see table of ranks). A former General Staff officer, Hausser was ideally suited to the task of licking the men of the armed SS units into shape, and when Hitler established the SS-*Verfügungstruppe* (SS-VT) Inspectorate on 1 October 1936, Hausser became its head. At this time the strength of the armed SS comprised the 2,660

SS* and Army ranks with their British and American equivalents

SS	Army	Anglo-American equivalent
Reichsführer-SS (Himmler)	No equivalent	No equivalent
Oberstgruppenführer	Generalfeldmarschall	Field Marshal (Br); 5-Star General (US)
Obergruppenführer	Generaloberst	General
Gruppenführer	General der Infanterie, Kavallerie or Artillerie	General (Br); Lt-General (US)
Brigadeführer	Generalleutnant	Lt-General (Br); Major-General (US)
Oberführer	Generalmajor	Major-General (Br); Brigadier (US)
Standartenführer	Oberst	Colonel
Obersturmbannführer	Oberstleutnant	Lt-Colonel
Sturmbannführer	Major	Major
Hauptsturmführer	Hauptmann	Captain
Obersturmführer	Oberleutnant	Lieutenant
Untersturmführer	Leutnant	2nd Lieutenant
Sturmscharführer	Hauptfeldwebel	Regimental Sergeant-Major (Br); First Sergeant (US)
Hauptscharführer	Oberfeldwebel	Sergeant Major (Br); Master Sergeant (US)
Oberscharführer	Feldwebel	Company Sergeant-Major (Br); Technical Sergeant (US)
Scharführer	Unterfeldwebel	Sergeant (Br); Staff Sergeant (US)
Unterscharführer	Unteroffizier	Sergeant
Rottenführer	Obergefreiter	Corporal
Sturmann	Gefreiter	Lance Corporal (Br); Acting Corporal (US)
Oberschütze	Oberschütze	Private (Br); PFC (US)
Mann	Schütze	Private

* As well as having different names for ranks, the Waffen-SS also titled its formations differently to their Army equivalents, a practice modelled on the original SA structure. The basic tactical unit was the *Sturm* (Company), commanded by an Unter- or Obersturmführer. Each Sturm was composed of three or four *Truppen* (Troops) under the

men of the Leibstandarte *Adolf Hitler*, 5,040 men in the two SS-VT regiments *Deutschland* and *Germania*, the 759 men attached to the two training schools and the 3,500 men in Eicke's five *Totenkopf* Sturmbanne. The latter were not officially recognized as part of the SS-VT because the Army refused to accept service in the *Totenkopfverbände* as the equivalent of military service, a bone of contention which Eicke only eventually overcame with difficulty.

From this small beginning, the Waffen-SS would, regardless of the obstacles in its path, eventually grow to an army of some 910,000 men. At its height the Waffen-SS never exceeded about 10 per cent of the Army's own strength, so was never the threat to the armed forces which the SA had been seen to be. Nevertheless, having eliminated one obstacle to cordial relations with the Army, Hitler — and Himmler — still had to prove that the armed SS was not a challenge to the Army's supposedly sole responsibility as arms bearers for the State. In a secret memo of 1935 Hitler wrote, 'In time of war the SS-VT will be incorporated into the Army'. Left unspoken was the real reason Hitler tolerated and even encouraged the expansion of an armed SS. Remembering the turbulence and violence throughout Germany at the end of the First World War, he foresaw that such a force, owing allegiance only to himself, could well be needed to quell civil disorder.

Later, on 17 August 1938 he clarified the situation in a further document which stated that in time of national emergency the SS-VT would be used for two purposes: 'By the Commander-in-Chief of the Army within the framework of the Army. It will then be subject exclusively to military law and instructions; politically, however, it will remain a branch of the NSDAP'; and, 'At home, in accordance with my instructions, it will then be under the orders of the Reichsführer-SS'.

Before this though what was needed was a 'spring clean' within the SS itself, for in its explosive growth after Hitler became Chancellor large numbers of men had been accepted for membership who fell far short of Himmler's ideals. If the SS was to be regarded as an elite, then those standards had to be reimposed. Thousands of men were therefore expelled between the time of the Röhm purge and the reintroduction of

---

command of a senior NCO, while each Truppe itself consisted of three *Scharen* (Squads) of eight men apiece. Going up the scale, three Stürme constituted a *Sturmbann* (Battalion), commanded by a Sturmbannführer; three Sturmbanne made a *Standarte* (Regiment), under a Standartenführer. Above this, individual composition varied but a number of Standarten would form a Brigade under a Brigadeführer or a *Gruppe* (Division) under a Gruppenführer. (The term 'Gruppe' was soon abandoned in favour of 'Division', to prevent confusion. Similarly, although the word *Obergruppen* existed, to designate a group of Divisions commanded by an Obergruppenführer or Oberstgruppenführer, the more normal Army word *Korps* (Corps) was usually used. Just to confuse things further, the Wehrmacht used the words *Kampfgruppe*, or 'battle group', to designate a formation generally larger than a Brigade but smaller than a Division, and *Heeresgruppe*, or Army Group, to denote a number of Korps.)

A member of a First World War Stosstruppe *festooned with grenades, rifle and even a shield reminiscent of those used in medieval times for hand-to-hand combat. It was on the experiences of such soldiers that Felix Steiner based the training manuals for the Waffen-SS.*

conscription, leaving a nucleus of dedicated personnel who fulfilled the necessary racial, physical and moral requirements. As an extreme example of the thoroughness of this selection process, Himmler said that for a period a volunteer would not be accepted into the SS-VT if he had had a single tooth filled!

Training was no less rigorous than the initial selection of suitable candidates. The guiding light in this was Felix Steiner, first commander of the *Deutschland* Standarte. As a junior infantry officer during the First World War, Steiner had been involved in the formation of the *Stosstruppen*, or assault troops, who pioneered what would now be regarded as commando–style tactics. Composed entirely of volunteers, the *Stosstruppen* were light infantry who went into action unencumbered by the usual backpack, festooned instead with grenades, sometimes tied together in bundles for greater effectiveness. A variety of improvised weapons was also introduced, including spades with sharpened blades to serve as battleaxes, while right at the end of the war the MP 18 sub-machine-gun began entering service. This fast-firing weapon, smaller than a rifle, was ideal in the close confines of trench warfare. The men of the *Stosstruppen* threw out the old concept of the massed infantry attack straight into the muzzles of the machine-guns which wreaked such carnage. Instead, they usually operated by night, crawling across No Man's Land, cutting through the barbed wire to leap suddenly into an enemy trench, create as much havoc

Above *The Waffen-SS emphasized physical fitness more than any other branch of the German armed forces. Here a group of young athletes discuss a sporting event.*

Right *Skill and co-ordination are principal requirements for any combat soldier.*

Although duelling was frowned upon and officially illegal in the Third Reich, fencing was a popular sport for SS men. Reinhard Heydrich was a master swordsman and set the example for many.

Waffen-SS training encouraged aggressiveness and mock trench raids and individual combats with clubbed rifle and bayonet were designed to nurture this spirit.

Above *Accuracy in shooting was equally important, and here officer candidates practise their skills at Bad Tölz (whose modern buildings are now garrisoned by the US Army!).*

Right *The men of the Verfügungstruppen had to be extremely fit to endure this sort of obstacle course.*

as possible then quietly disappear before the demoralized survivors could rally for a counter-attack. This, Steiner thought, should be the style of the SS-VT; let the Army provide the cannon fodder.

Hausser and Steiner had good material to work with in the first place. Despite the fact that nearly half the SS recruits had received only minimal schooling — at officer candidate level lower than the standard demanded by the Army — their physical fitness and motivation were both high. Himmler himself was able to boast in 1937 that 'we still choose only fifteen out of every hundred candidates who present themselves'. Moreover, to be eligible for a commission, officer candidates had to have served for at least two years in the ranks. Officers enlisted for 25 years, NCOs for 12 and privates for four, but basic training was the same for all.

A recruit's day began at 6 am with a rigorous hour's PT, followed by a breakfast of porridge and mineral water! The morning continued with intensive weapons training, target practice and unarmed combat sessions, interrupted three times a week by ideological lectures in which both Party doctrine and 'Aryan' supremacy featured heavily. A hearty lunch was followed by a drill session, then a period of scrubbing, cleaning, scouring and polishing, and finally a cross-country run or a couple of hours on the sports field. If a recruit had any energy left after all this, he might be able to acquire a pass, but even this involved a close inspection to ensure that every aspect of his uniform was immaculate and that he was freshly bathed and shaved. The general preference was for something else to eat and an early night.

Unlike the Army, whose basic training stressed drill and then more drill, SS training emphasized fighting skills and physical toughness.* Another difference was that Steiner made a serious attempt to break down the rigid class division which traditionally existed between officers and men. Officers and NCOs were encouraged to get to know their men off-duty as individuals, personnel of all ranks addressing each other as *kamerad* (comrade). This did not, to the surprise of many Army officers, lead to breakdown of discipline, since a soldier who knows that his officers care is generally more reliable than one who does not. Similarly, if he understands his orders he is usually able to carry them out more intelligently than if he is following them blindly. Instead of turning out military marionettes, Steiner intended to produce soldiers who were *self*-disciplined and self-reliant, and to a large degree he succeeded. The small size of the pre-war SS-VT compared to the Army obviously helped, and encouraged individual tuition, but the standards of training *Germanic* recruits stayed at a high level almost until the end. We shall look at the rather different status of foreign volunteers later.

Following basic training and the administration of the oath, advanced

---

* Because of their ceremonial duties as formal guards for the Reich Chancellery and at parades, etc, the Leibstandarte *Adolf Hitler* suffered from a greater deal of parade ground bashing and general routine than the other regiments. This, and not the colour of their dress uniform (see page 47), earned them the unappreciated title 'asphalt soldiers'.

The troops of the Leibstandarte Adolf Hitler earned themselves the unwelcome nickname of 'asphalt soldiers' because of their many ceremonial duties. In the photo above Hitler himself inspects a billet while below the motor cycle reconnaissance company is drawn up in formation on a football pitch.

training at one of the infantry or cavalry schools — the SS-VT possessed no artillery in the early days — took a rather different course, although the emphasis on sporting activity was maintained. Now it was designed to teach a soldier who knew elementary weapons how to behave and react on the battlefield. There is no substitute for realism, and Steiner and Hausser introduced live firing exercises for the SS-VT in which real rather than blank ammunition was used. This is just one of many Waffen-SS practices which has been more or less universally adopted subsequently, but at the time it attracted considerable criticism from Army pundits who complained at the inevitable casualties. Even when someone is not deliberately trying to kill you, a bullet has to go *somewhere*. In the long run, though, such exercises almost certainly saved lives because once they went to war the men of the SS-VT were not unnerved by the simple fact of being under fire, and could thus react more coolly, without panic or uncertainty.*

Once the German Army acquired tanks — even though to begin with they were just cars with plywood hulls used for training — the exercises went further. Recruits had to dig themselves foxholes in front of advancing vehicles, shelter in them while they clattered overhead, then leap out to hurl practice grenades at them. In fact, one apocryphal story even has it that as a test of courage SS-VT men had to stand rigidly at attention while a grenade was balanced on top of their steel helmets and the pin pulled!

After this year at training school recruits passed out as fully fledged soldiers of the SS and newly commissioned officers graduating from Bad Tölz and Braunschweig received their daggers. At the same time all ranks had to take the SS marriage oath; this committed them to obtaining permission from RuSHA before getting married, and RuSHA would examine the prospective bride's pedigree before giving consent. This often took a long time and young people get impatient, so despite knowing that they could be expelled from the SS for marrying without permission, many did so regardless. As in other things Himmler eventually found the whole Nordic or 'Aryan' interbreeding system unworkable and many men who had been dismissed from the SS for marrying without official sanction were later re-admitted.

There was a very pragmatic reason for this and other later concessions. Himmler was as much a power-seeker as Göring and other prominent Nazis, and grew to realize that he had to rely upon manpower in order to secure his position. In this he was hampered by the Army's attitude towards the SS, which had been congratulatory over the Röhm purge but which had cooled since Hindenburg died. At that point Hitler had

---

* Nevertheless, when war did come, it was found that the casualty rate among fighting SS formations averaged higher than in the Army. The usual explanations given are that SS troops were more aggressive, that they were trying to prove themselves better than Army troops, and that they were handed the stickiest assignments. There is truth in all three assertions, especially the last when applied to the Russian Front. In the early days of the war, though, much of the loss rate was due simply to inexperienced leadership.

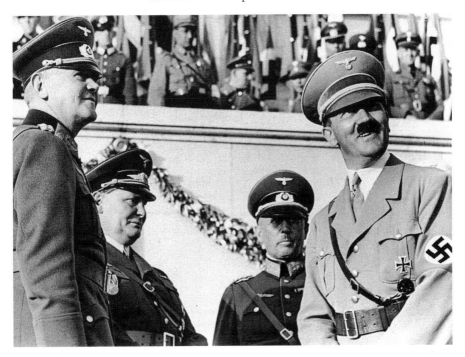

While Göring and von Fritsch look serious, von Blomberg appears to be enjoying a joke with his Führer in this photo taken at Nürnberg in 1937.

suspended the Presidency and chosen the new title 'Führer and Chancellor' to whom members of the armed forces then had to swear allegiance. A couple of months later he introduced the new SS oath, quoted on page 25, and thereby established an armed force independent of all others and owing allegiance only to himself. He then placed the SS-VT *and* the *Totenkopfverbände* on the police budget (1 April 1936) and this, coupled with Göring's and Himmler's gradual absorption of ever greater control over the German police force, was not something the Generals could take lightly (despite the even more rapid expansion of the regular armed forces since 1935). They therefore had to be put in their place just as the SA had been so that the SS could assume its 'rightful place in the sun'.

In 1933 Hitler had approved the appointment of General Werner von Blomberg, one of his staunchest supporters in the Army, as Minister of Defence, and later promoted him to Field Marshal. The following year he made General Freiherr Werner von Fritsch Commander-in-Chief of the Army. Both men supported Hitler personally because they saw in him the man who could restore the Army's prestige, and Blomberg gradually introduced steps to 'Nazify' the armed forces, prohibiting marriage with non-Aryans, ordering that uniformed members of the various NSDAP organizations should be saluted and refusing commissions to officer

Blomberg and Fritsch were both concerned at the German occupation of Austria in 1938, but many people were enthusiastic at the two countries' drawing closer together. The euphoria would not last.

candidates who did not publicly support the Party. Fritsch himself was not a Nazi and in particular was suspicious of the SS although he applauded the role they had played in the Röhm purge. However, neither Blomberg nor Fritsch was happy in March 1936 when the German Army was ordered to reoccupy the Rhineland, which had been demilitarized under the terms of the Treaty of Versailles. Even though the feared French military response failed to materialize, the two men were concerned because the Army was far from being in any fit state for war.

Their concern deepened throughout the period of the *Anschluss* ('Joining') in March 1938 when German troops, including the SS-VT, marched into Austria at the request of the Minister of the Interior, Dr Arthur Seyss-Inquart. Seyss-Inquart was a closet Nazi who had deliberately fomented civil disorder using Ernst Kaltenbrunner's Austrian SS units, then appealed to Berlin for 'help'.* The Austrian Chancellor, Kurt

---

* Kaltenbrunner became head of the RSHA after Heydrich's assassination in 1942, was arrested at the end of the war and hanged in 1946. Seyss-Inquart later played an unsavoury role in the German administration of first Poland and then Holland, earning the undying hatred of the Dutch people for his brutality. He, too, was hanged at Nürnberg in 1946.

Schuschnigg, who had valiantly tried to oppose Hitler, joined some 76,000 fellow countrymen in concentration camps. The *Anschluss*, though, was generally regarded by the outside world as a purely German affair. Czechoslovakia was a totally different matter.

Hitler had outlined his plans for Austria and Czechoslovakia during a conference held in November 1937 at which, along with Blomberg and Fritsch, Göring (as head of the *Luftwaffe*, or Air Force), Admiral Erich Raeder (C-in-C of the *Kriegsmarine*, or Navy), and Freiherr Constantin von Neurath (the Foreign Minister) were also present. The Hossbach Conference, as it was called after the officer who took the meeting's notes, had actually been called by Blomberg and Raeder to discuss rearmament, but Hitler used it as a platform for his ideas on *Lebensraum*. The annexation of Austria and Czechoslovakia would provide enough food for an estimated six million German people as well as manpower for an extra 12 Army divisions, he said. The Czech armaments industry was also one of the most innovative and productive in Europe and would be able to contribute a great deal to the *Wehrmacht* (an all-embracing term for the armed forces

Fritsch in the centre with Blomberg on his left and General Gerd von Rundstedt on his right. Rundstedt was forced into retirement at the same time that the other two men were 'removed' but was recalled to help plan the invasion of Poland and commanded Army Group A in 1940 (see later). He was dismissed a second time during the Russian campaign but again reinstated, as commander of all the forces in the west in 1944, then sacked for the third time in March 1945. He died in 1953.

General von Brauchitsch was dismissed after the army's failure to capture Moscow in 1941 but Jodl (centre) and Keitel held on to the reins of power to the bitter end. Here, Göring appears to be lecturing both of them. The date is some time after the July 1944 bomb plot because Jodl is wearing his specially minted Wound Badge.

excluding the SS). But all Blomberg, Fritsch and Neurath could see was the disastrous possibility of a war on two fronts if France and/or Britain decided to intervene over Czechoslovakia. Despite their protestations, the dictator was adamant, regarding their fears as cowardly, and from this point onwards began to plan the replacement of the three men by others who would be more tractable.

Freiherr von Neurath was the easiest to remove, and subsequently held only relatively minor posts; he was given a prison sentence at Nürnberg but released because of ill health in 1954 and died two years later. He was replaced by Joachim Ribbentrop, former ambassador to London and the man largely responsible for two important anti-Communist treaties with Japan and Italy (the Anti-Comintern Pacts of 1936 and '37). Getting rid of the two Generals was more difficult and necessitated resort to blackmail, but was essential to the Führer's plans and, almost incidentally, to the growth of the armed SS.

In 1938 Field Marshal von Blomberg, whose first wife had died six years earlier, remarried to a young lady called Erna Grün. Unfortunately Göring, who had initially supported the match, discovered that she had once posed for pornographic photographs. Faced with the evidence, the sixty-year-old Field Marshal was forced to resign. He retired into obscurity and died in

1946. Next to go was General von Fritsch. Heydrich's SD fabricated information that he had been seen associating with a male prostitute, and he was cashiered from the Army even though a secret internal enquiry subsequently established his innocence.* Hitler replaced von Fritsch with the sycophantic General Walter von Brauchitsch and abolished the Ministry of Defence, creating a new armed forces high command (OKW — *Oberkommando der Wehrmacht*) with himself as its head and two more 'yes men', General Wilhelm 'lickspittle' Keitel (the nickname was given to him by the British Press during the war) and Alfred Jodl, as Chief of Staff and Chief of Operations respectively.† Now Hitler finally had supreme executive command over all the armed forces.

One of his first acts was to clarify and rationalize the status of the SS-VT in the proclamation quoted on page 35. He also declared members of the *Allgemeine* (General) SS immune from conscription (but free to volunteer), thereby at one stroke smoothing the path to eventual military recognition of Eicke's three *Totenkopf* Standarten. At the same time he instructed that the SS-VT was henceforth to wear the same field grey uniform as the Army (except that the Leibstandarte continued to wear black for ceremonial occasions), but retaining their own distinctive rank insignia and helmet decals. None of these moves seemed to cause the Army any concern. Although the SS-VT had been enlarged since the *Anschluss* by a fourth Standarte, *Der Führer* (based in Vienna and Klagenfurt), its rigid selection procedures meant that the SS was only skimming off a tiny fraction of the recruits needed by the Wehrmacht. In time of war, it was planned that reserves would be drawn from the *Totenkopfverbände*.

Returning to the Czech question, Hitler's first objective was the Sudetenland, the stretch of land lying between Bohemia and Silesia which had been tacked on to Bohemia and Moravia to make the new country of Czechoslovakia in 1919. Its population was predominantly German-speaking and the pro-Nazi Nationalist Party under Konrad Henlein had been agitating for reunification with Germany since 1933. Britain and France had 'guaranteed' Czech independence and international tensions ran high during August 1938 in two meetings between Hitler and British Prime Minister Neville Chamberlain. Finally, at a third meeting in München in September which was also attended by the Italian dictator Benito Mussolini and French Premier Edouard Daladier, the four leaders agreed to accede to the Sudeten Germans' requests and Hitler's demands. The Sudetenland was ceded to Germany without a shot being fired and Chamberlain returned to London with his infamous 'peace in our time' speech. But Hitler's ambitions did not stop there.

In March 1939 the German Army marched unopposed into

---

* As a result, when war came Fritsch was allowed to take over honorary Colonelcy of his old regiment and died in action in Poland in 1939.

† Both survived the various purges Hitler subsequently made in the top ranks of the officer corps, only to be hanged at Nürnberg.

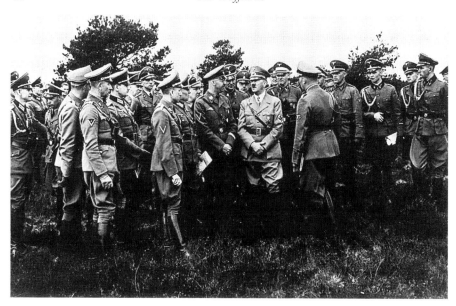

Hitler watching the Deutschland *Standarte's demonstration at Munsterlager in the summer of 1939. Alongside him are Himmler and Obergruppenführer Karl Wolff. Paul Hausser is in the left foreground of the picture.*

Bohemia/Moravia while Britain and France stood uselessly by. Czech President Eduard Beneš fled to London to head the government in exile. Three of the SS-VT Standarten — Leibstandarte *Adolf Hitler*, *Deutschland* and *Germania* — as well as the *Totenkopf* Standarte *Oberbayern*, took part in the invasion. Then, dressed in the mottle camouflage smocks which were to become one of their distinctive trademarks, the *Deutschland* Standarte gave a demonstration of an infantry assault SS-style in front of Hitler during the summer. The speed and ferocity of their attack — in which live ammunition was used — greatly impressed Hitler, and he finally authorized the formation of a fully-fledged SS-VT division with an integral artillery Standarte. Before this order could be completely implemented, though, Germany was at war with Poland.

3

Victories and growth 1939-41

The SS formations did not have an independent role during the invasion of Poland which began on 1 September 1939, nor was the lightning eighteen-day campaign a real test of their abilities. Standarte *Deutschland*, together with the new SS artillery regiment and reconnaissance battalion, was brigaded with the 7th and 8th Panzer Regiments in a battlegroup commanded by General Werner Kempf, and took part in the fierce fight for Brest-Litovsk. *Germania* was held in reserve with Fourteenth Army but saw some action in the Lemberg region. The Leibstandarte *Adolf Hitler*, attached to the 17th Infantry Division, saw the toughest fighting. Being a motorized formation — whereas most Army units were still horse-drawn — it was used largely in the reconnaissance and flank defence roles and saw heavy fighting around Pabianice. The Leibstandarte was then re-allocated to 4th Panzer Division and fought its way through Lodz into the outskirts of Warsaw before being moved west to take part in the first encirclement manoeuvre of the war in the bend of the River Bzura. The newly formed Standarte *Der Führer* did not participate in the campaign, and only one *Totenkopf* Sturmbann saw any action. Men of both this unit and the new artillery regiment were accused by the Army of atrocities including the wanton killing of civilians (ie, Jews), and a few SS men were subsequently court martialled but, under pressure from the top, given very lenient prison sentences.

If the Army was not impressed by the performance of the SS-V units (the 'T' for *Truppen* had been dropped by this time) because of their high casualty rate as well as the needless murders, Hitler was proud of them and almost immediately the Polish campaign was over authorized their expansion into three full divisions. Moreover, to prevent any more 'embarrassing incidents', in October Hitler freed the armed SS from Wehrmacht judicial jurisdiction, decreeing that henceforth miscreants accused by the Army of misconduct could only be tried by specially appointed SS courts. (The reverse side of this coin is that full-time members

Machine-gun crew of an unidentified SS unit during the invasion of Poland. Many Army officers ridiculed their mottle camouflage smocks at the time but in fact the SS pioneered the style of personal camouflage which has become almost universal in modern armies.

of the *Heer* (Army), *Kriegsmarine* (Navy) and *Luftwaffe* (Air Force) were supposedly immune from the SS and Gestapo, who could only report them to their own superior officers. This quid pro quo altered as the war dragged on though, until eventually Himmler's men could arrest, question and, if necessary, execute virtually anyone on their own authority... and often did.)

The SS-*Verfügungsdivision* merely needed casualties replacing to bring it back up to strength, and this was achieved out of the jealously restricted manpower quota which the Army allowed the armed SS. The problem was partially overcome by recruiting ethnic Germans from the Sudetenland and the new 'Protectorate' of Bohemia and Moravia, the beginning of a trend which would ultimately result in there being more non-German than German-born men in the armed SS. The Leibstandarte *Adolf Hitler*, lavishly equipped with the most modern vehicles and weapons as befitted Hitler's bodyguard, was increased to the size of a reinforced regiment. The *Totenkopf* Standarten were also motorized and brought up to approximately the same strength as the SS-V Division, but were still not regarded by the Army as a proper military formation and were paid out of the Interior

Ministry budget. It would take another six months before these anomalies would be resolved.

Meanwhile Himmler, having received permission to create a third division, had the problem of finding the men to fill it. This he accomplished by drafting thousands of ordinary policemen (*Ordnungspolizei*), many of them middle aged, with a leavening of younger men from the *Totenkopfverbände* and volunteers from the *Allgemeine* SS, to form the Polizei Division. This remained a poor grade unit throughout the war, its personnel lacking the physical and ideological qualities of the original armed SS formations. Moreover, many of its personnel resented being taken away from their chosen professions to act as soldiers. These differences in quality were recognized by Himmler and although the Polizei Division wore field grey uniforms they bore police instead of SS insignia.

After months of wrangling the OKW was finally persuaded to accept the *Totenkopf* as part of the armed SS and on 2 March 1940 the title 'Waffen-SS' at last became official. However, members of the *Totenkopfverbände*, although they could be called upon as a reserve manpower pool, were still regarded as second-class citizens and the Army refused to accept

Alfred Wünnenberg, later CO of the Polizei Division, illustrating the totally different cap and collar patch insignia worn by the men of this formation.

concentration camp duty as the equivalent of military service. This situation was never actually resolved but eventually became meaningless as the war imposed even heavier demands for more and more men.

Manpower was not Himmler's only problem; if his divisions were to function properly they needed their own integral artillery battalions, but there was already an acute shortage of guns due to the expansion of the Army itself. The Leibstandarte, naturally, received nothing but the best, and the Polizei Division (which was not expected to play an active role in the assault on France and the Low Countries) could make do with obsolescent horse-drawn weapons. The *Verfügungsdivision* already had an artillery regiment, of course, but there was reluctance to give the SS *Totenkopf* Division the equipment it needed. Moreover, being motorized it would also require extra vehicles to haul its guns, and these were in equally short supply. Eventually the Army high command agreed with ill grace that it could be equipped with Czech weapons — which were actually every bit as good as home-grown German ones* — but only after the needs of the Army's own front-line formations had been satisfied. This meant that deliveries were extremely slow to come through, and the wrangling over priorities for the Waffen-SS would continue throughout the May/June campaigns in the west.

Nevertheless, the American historian George H. Stein makes an interesting comment about the *Totenkopf* Division as it stood poised for action in April 1940, and the following quote is taken verbatim from his authoritative book *The Waffen-SS: Hitler's elite guard at war 1939–1945* (see *Further reading*). The division had been assigned to General Max Weichs's Second Army for the assault in the west and on 4 April he paid his first visit to Eicke's command.

'In their opening conversation with Eicke, Weichs and his staff revealed their ignorance about the new division that had been added to their command. They were under the impression that the *Totenkopf* Division was "organized and equipped like a Czech foot division", and were very much surprised to discover it was really a modern, motorized infantry division. At a time when only seven of the German Army's 139 infantry divisions were motorized this was indeed a command to be proud of. And when Eicke added the information that a heavy artillery section was being organized for the division, Weichs' professional interest was aroused and his coolness began to dissipate. Weichs' inspection of the troops left him visibly impressed, and he completed his visit in a frame of mind far different from that in which he had arrived.'

(Weichs was not the only Army officer to regard the *Totenkopf* Division with high respect. Field Marshal Erich von Manstein, one of Germany's ablest senior officers during the war, later came to consider it the finest unit under his command.)

* In fact 25 per cent of the German Army's tanks in 1940 were Czech PzKpfw 35 and '38(t)s.

* * *

In terms of military activity, the six months following the collapse of Poland (divided by prior arrangement into a German and a Russian zone) were quiet. Although Britain and France had both declared war on 3 September 1939 they made no attempt to attack Germany other than by means of intermittent bombing raids. There were a few naval actions, but on land there was an uneasy lull — the 'Phoney War' or, as the Germans called it, *Sitzkrieg*, a pun on *Blitzkrieg* ('lightning war'). Behind the scenes though there was frantic activity as reserves were called up and recruiting stations were swamped by volunteers. In Germany it was a time to mull over the lessons which had been learned both in Poland and by the Condor Legion which had fought on General Francisco Franco's side during the Spanish Civil War (1936–9). Then the peace was shattered on 9 April 1940 when German forces, including paras and alpine troops, invaded Denmark and Norway. Denmark surrendered immediately but fighting continued in Norway for two months.

No Waffen-SS units took part in these operations but they were to have a significant role in *Fall Gelb* (Case Yellow), German code–name for the invasion of the west. The basic German scheme was to draw British and French troops north by a right hook down through Holland and Belgium, then to smash them in the flank and rear by an assault using the cream of the Panzer divisions through the Ardennes, which the Allies considered impassable to tanks. The SS divisions assembled for the attack were; in the north, with Army Group B, the Leibstandarte and SS-V Division; in the

Men of the Totenkopf *Division cross a stream under fire during the campaign in the west.*

Totenkopf *personnel come under artillery fire.*

centre with OKW reserve behind Army Group A, the *Totenkopf*; and in the south, facing the Maginot Line, the Polizei Division in Army Group C.

During the night of 9/10 May the Leibstandarte and *Der Führer* regiments moved up to their start lines on the Dutch border, their task being to effect a link with the airborne troops who would be dropped at dawn to seize vital bridges and airfields. As day broke the Leibstandarte overpowered the Dutch border guards while wave after wave of Junkers Ju 87 Stuka dive-bombers thundered overhead. Racing 50 miles (80 km) in the first six hours, the men of the Leibstandarte reached their first objective, Zwolle, only to find that the Dutch army had demolished the bridge there. Undeterred, the SS men built improvised rafts to cross the River Yssel until engineers could effect more permanent arrangements, and pushed forward a further 50 miles that day, the first much publicized Iron Cross of the campaign being awarded to Obersturmführer Hugo Krass. At the same time, *Der Führer* spearheaded the advance of the 227th Infantry Division near Arnhem, becoming involved in heavy fighting for the Grebbe Line, while the rest of the SS-V Division surged forward alongside the 9th Panzer Division towards Moerdijk, where paras *had* seized the bridge. A French threat to their flank caused them to abandon this objective, which was entrusted to the Leibstandarte instead, but the French were repulsed and 9th Panzer charged on towards Rotterdam, leaving the SS-V to mop up behind them. Following the infamous bombing of the city — an operation which was actually cancelled because the city surrendered but which went ahead anyway because most of the bombers failed to receive the recall signal in time — the SS units headed for The Hague. By the time they reached this objective, though, Holland had capitulated leaving just the naval garrison in Zeeland still fighting. The *Deutschland* Regiment was moved up with heavy Luftwaffe support to subdue them but the Dutch forces were evacuated to England by sea.

Meanwhile the *Totenkopf* Division had been taken out of reserve and ordered into Belgium to join the XV Panzer Korps. They reached the position held by General Erwin Rommel's 7th Panzer Division at Le Cateau on the 19th and were thrown straight into the fray. Next day the British launched a strong counter-attack with 74 Matilda tanks supported by some 60 assorted French tanks and two battalions of infantry. This was the first real check to the headlong German advance and the Allied tanks were only beaten back because Rommel moved his 8.8 cm anti-aircraft guns up and deployed them in the anti-tank role. (These at the time were the only German anti-tank guns capable of destroying a Matilda.) Nevertheless, the battle was 'a close run thing'.

Totenkopf pressed onwards towards Merville, suffering such high casualties that the XV Panzer Korps commander, General Hermann Hoth, accused Eicke of being 'a butcher and no soldier'. Butchery, indeed, was to follow although the full story did not emerge until after the war. The 4th Company of the division's 2nd Standarte, commanded by Obersturmführer Fritz Knochlein, was held up by the determined resistance of an isolated group of about 100 soldiers from the 2nd Royal Norfolk Regiment. Retreating through the little hamlet of Le Paradis, the Norfolks first tried to hold out in a farmhouse but were forced to retire when it was set alight by mortar fire. Realizing further resistance was useless, the men — who had attempted to find cover in a cowshed — raised

SS machine-gun crew in a camouflaged position during the fighting in France.

Officers of the Standarte Germania *confer during the French campaign.*

a white flag. They were marched along a lane to a barn outside which two machine-guns had been set up. Lined up in front of it, they were mercilessly gunned down, survivors being finished off with the bayonet. Miraculously, two men escaped, concealed beneath the pile of bodies, but both were wounded and later gave themselves up to a regular Army unit to prevent reprisals against the villagers. One of the men was repatriated in 1943 as a result of his injuries but his story was not believed until his companion was released at the end of the war. Knochlein was later recognized in Hamburg by a villager from Le Paradis, brought to trial in 1948 and executed.

Unfortunately, *Totenkopf* was not the only SS unit to be responsible for a massacre during this campaign. The Leibstandarte was by this time moving up towards the Dunkirk perimeter, within which thousands of men from the British Expeditionary Force (BEF) were awaiting evacuation. Outside the village of Wormhoudt, the car in which the regiment's commander, 'Sepp' Dietrich, was being driven came under heavy fire and burst into flames. He flung himself into a culvert for shelter, rolling in the mud to protect himself from the heat, but it was to be five hours before German troops eliminated the resistance and rescued him.

Incensed at the thought that their bluff, crude but beloved commander had been killed, the Leibstandarte threw themselves at the defenders of Wormhoudt, some 330 men from the 2nd Royal Warwickshire and Cheshire Regiments and the Royal Artillery. About 80 men were taken prisoner by a company from the regiment's 2nd Sturmbann, whose own commander had been badly wounded. They were herded into a barn whereupon their guards started throwing hand grenades, shooting down those who tried to escape. Someone finally called a halt to the slaughter but there were only 15 survivors. Again, the story did not emerge until after the war, but this time not one of the culprits was identified until in 1988 *The Sunday Times* unearthed a previously censored wartime report and revealed the officer in charge as having been Hauptsturmführer Wilhelm Mohnke, by then an elderly retired businessman living near Hamburg.

It is, of course, popular to portray the Waffen-SS as the perpetrators of all the worst combat atrocities, although most people admit that the Russians were just as bad or worse — the Katyn massacre discussed later is ample testimony to this. But no army is completely innocent of such incidents, and I know personally one former Royal Tank Regiment officer who has admitted in writing that he and his men mowed down the occupants of a German bunker in Italy after they had shown a white flag and emerged with their hands in the air. Anger at the loss of friends and comrades is a natural emotion and after days or weeks in the field normal human sensibilities are dulled. The reason such stories rarely emerge in respect of the conduct of the Allied forces is the usual one: to the victors the spoils, and it is the victors who generally write the history books. I *would* have liked to reprint here a letter I received from a veteran of the US 82nd Airborne Division in this context, but it is unfortunately unprintable and does that illustrious

The speed of the campaign exhausted the men, as well as wearing out many of their vehicles.

Above *During a lull, men of the Verfügungsdivision clean and check their weapons.*

Below *At the end of the campaign, Paul Hausser awards medals to those men of his division who had particularly distinguished themselves.*

In jovial mood, Himmler congratulates 'Sepp' Dietrich on the Leibstandarte's performance.

unit no credit. None of this in any way, though, vindicates the actions of the Waffen-SS in the above mentioned or other later incidents.

After being pulled out of the line for a brief rest, the Leibstandarte was first attached to General Ewald von Kleist's Panzergruppe then to XLIV Korps which was rapidly heading towards the River Marne. They were joined by the *Totenkopf* Division shortly afterwards. By this time (10 June) French resistance was rapidly crumbling and the advance became headlong, with the Leibstandarte in the lead as often as not. By 24 June the weary SS men had reached St Etienne where they halted because a ceasefire came into effect next day. Similarly, the SS-V Division had been pulled out of Holland on 18 May and also seconded to von Kleist's Panzergruppe. After taking part in the battle for Arras the division was next attached to General Walter von Reichenau's Sixth Army, subsequently going in with the second wave of the attack on the Weygand Line on 5 June. After crossing the River Somme, the SS-V broke through to the rear of the French positions and were soon on the road through Soissons towards Troyes. Their last battle of the campaign took place on 16 June when they blocked French troops trying to flee westwards from the Maginot Line, and from then until the ceasefire on 25 June it was a matter of hot pursuit against minimal resistance.

Despite the atrocities — which no one except those responsible and the handful of survivors knew about at the time — the Waffen-SS formations had acquitted themselves well in their first proper campaign and both

Hitler and Himmler were delighted with them. The commanders of the Leibstandarte *Adolf Hitler*, 'Sepp' Dietrich, the *Deutschland*, Felix Steiner, and the *Der Führer*, Georg Keppler, were each awarded the Knights Cross of the Iron Cross. Further expansion of the Waffen-SS was to be another reward for the 'playboy soldier', Himmler, and his associates.

*   *   *

Once Himmler, through his principal recruiting officer, Gottlob Berger, had opened up the SS to people of Germanic blood living outside Germany itself, he at one fell swoop circumvented the restrictions on growth imposed by the Army (and, latterly, by the Air Force as well, for Göring was also demanding manpower for the new Luftwaffe Field Divisions he was intent on creating). By the summer of 1940 the Waffen-SS divisions had already accepted a number of volunteers from neutral Sweden and Switzerland, from Romania and even half a dozen from the United States, many of whose citizens are, of course, of German descent. Following the conquest of the West, the gates were opened to an initial trickle and later a flood of volunteers from the occupied countries.

One question always asked is why anyone, be he German or, especially, of another nationality, should have wanted to join the Waffen-SS in the first place. The first concept to dismiss is that they were all just thugs attracted by a stylish uniform, although, inevitably, there were a fair proportion of those. We have already seen how strong the appeal of blood — of race — was in 1930s Germany, and to many the SS epitomized those 'ideals'. And if the SS as a whole was presented (and regarded itself) as an elite, its armed branch was even more so. Recruits for the SS came from all walks of life, from farm labourers to doctors, lawyers and members of the aristocracy and landed families. Generally, the level of educational attainment among those who joined the Waffen-SS was low, because it was to such people that the emotional attraction was greatest, the uniforms, pageantry and pseudo-mysticism the most appealing; the better educated tended to gravitate towards the SD. But throughout the ranks of the SS, it was the idea of belonging to an elite which was the main lure.

Even when you look at the *Totenkopfverbände* the same holds true, for in the early days a large number of people felt strongly that dissidents *should* be locked up in concentration camps and forced to work for the greater good of the nation rather than trying to tear down all that the NSDAP was achieving. Camp guard duty was, therefore, seen by many as a profession equally honourable to that of a regular prison warder. (This, of course, was before the camps became extermination centres, but by that time the majority of guards were conscripts not volunteers anyway. Moreover, when they experienced the reality of the camps, a large number of men, to their credit, did volunteer for the fighting formations instead, another point which is often glossed over.)

To answer the same question in respect of the non-Germans who flocked to join the Waffen-SS is more difficult. After the German invasion of Russia in June 1941 it becomes more understandable, because many people who were neither particularly pro-German nor pro-Nazi detested Communism and saw the Soviet Union as the gravest threat to Europe, so in one sense the Nazis' claim to be fighting an international crusade against Bolshevism was true. (The Belgian Rexist leader Léon Degrelle quoted later is particularly eloquent on this point.) But why, in 1940, within weeks of seeing their countries overrun, should hundreds of Norwegians, Danes, Belgians and Dutchmen have volunteered for service with the German armed forces? A fair proportion, inevitably, *were* politically motivated by an admiration for Hitler and his policies, and each of the occupied countries had its equivalent of the NSDAP, all with an anti-Semitic bias. However, the leaders of these parties generally opposed their members joining the German armed forces (wanting to keep control for themselves), and political motivation on its own does not account for the sheer number of volunteers. Part of the answer lies contradictorily in the fact of occupation itself. People had seen their own armies crumble in the face of the German divisions, and even in defeat could respect and admire sheer military virtuosity. The German troops, smart and well equipped, generally behaved decently towards the local populace, and rapidly began to be seen by many as 'not bad sorts'. (There were, of course, numerous exceptions to the rule, and resentment and resistance steadily mounted once the Gestapo and home-grown Nazi police forces such as the *Milice* in France took control.) One additional and very simple reason for the number of men joining up was the same one which over decades has attracted recruits for the French Foreign Legion: a primitive and atavistic desire for adventure.

Whatever, the first of the foreign volunteers were assigned to two new SS Standarten with German officers: *Nordland*, composed of Danes and Norwegians; and *Westland*, with Flemish and Dutch personnel. Then, in December 1940 Hitler authorized their expansion into a fourth Waffen-SS division. Standarte *Germania* was taken away from the SS-V Division to create the new division's cadre, and the parent division was brought back up to strength by forming a new (unnamed) Standarte from *Totenkopfverbände* personnel. The new division was originally named *Germania*, but it was felt that this did not properly reflect its cosmopolitan make-up and shortly afterwards it was renamed *Wiking*. Similarly, the SS-V Division was renamed *Deutschland*, but since this could have caused confusion with the Army's elite *Großdeutschland* Division in turn it was renamed *Reich*, later to become *Das Reich*. Command of the new division was entrusted to Felix Steiner while Paul Hausser assumed personal control of *Reich* in addition to his duties as Inspector-General of the Waffen-SS. Then, in spring 1941, two more *Totenkopf* Standarten were organized into a battlegroup under Karl Demelhuber (the original commander of Standarte *Germania*) which was given the name *Nord*. A third *Totenkopf* Standarte, the 9th, was posted to occupation duties in Norway under Army control. Meanwhile, the Leibstandarte *Adolf Hitler* was enlarged to the size of a reinforced brigade, still under 'Sepp' Dietrich, and it was with these forces that the Waffen-SS went to war in 1941.

They also had a new high command structure, equivalent to the OKH (*Oberkommando des Heeres*, or Army High Comand), the SSFHA (*SS Führungshauptamt* or 'high leading department'). This had been established by Himmler on 15 August 1940 to co-ordinate the military affairs of the SS and was administered personally by himself with the able assistance of his chief of staff, Hans Jüttner. Moreover, before the campaign in Russia began, Keitel had authorized the exchange of all Czech and other foreign weapons in the hands of the motorized SS formations for German weapons identical to those possessed by the Army and the creation of an assault gun battalion in each SS division.

There were, of course, problems of integration in the new *Wiking* Division quite apart from the obvious one of language. Having been promised equality with their German comrades-in-arms, many of the foreign volunteers found that things were actually rather different. Despite all Steiner's strenuous efforts to stamp out discrimination, there were numerous complaints about poorer rations, pay being docked for imaginary misdemeanours, of extra duties and cancelled leave. However, Steiner found it almost impossible totally to correct the many instances of injustice and instil his new division with the same sort of camaraderie as existed in the other Waffen-SS formations. This would only come in the maelstrom of the Russian Front, for it is impossible to discriminate against someone with whom you share a trench and depend upon to guard your back while fighting under the sort of conditions the German soldiery encountered in the Soviet Union.

4
Fire, mud and ice: the Balkans and Russia 1941-3

Despite the unholy alliance which had existed between Germany and Russia since the signing of the non-aggression pact in August 1939 and the carving up of Poland the following month, Hitler always saw the Soviet Union as Nazi Germany's principal enemy and began planning an attack the moment the campaign in the West was over. (Britain, of course, remained unsubdued but plans for an invasion, codenamed Operation *Seelöwe* (Sealion), had to be shelved and eventually abandoned after the Luftwaffe's failure to destroy the RAF in the Battle of Britain during July to September 1940. This meant, though, that approximately 60 German divisions were tied down in occupation duties in western Europe, Scandinavia and guarding the Channel coast against the possibility of British amphibious landings when they could have been more profitably deployed on the Eastern Front.)

On 18 December 1940 Führer Directive No 21 set out the objectives of the campaign, planned to be launched in May the following year. This Directive said that:

'The bulk of the Russian army stationed in western Russia will be destroyed by daring operations led by deeply penetrating armoured spearheads. Russian forces still capable of giving battle will be prevented from withdrawing into the depths of Russia.

'The enemy will then be energetically pursued and a line will be reached from which the Russian air force can no longer attack German territory. The final objective of the operation is to erect a barrier against Asiatic Russia on the general line Volga-Archangel. The last surviving industrial areas of Russia in the Urals can then, if necessary, be eliminated by the Luftwaffe.'

(In the wake of the Battle of Britain, more than one German officer privately expressed his doubts at the latter's capability, doubts which were to seem groundless at first during the initial sweeping victories, but were to later emerge as fully justified.)

To Hitler, and even more so to Himmler, the campaign against Russia *was* seen as a crusade, a crusade in which the Waffen-SS would play the role of latter-day Teutonic Knights. Shortly after German troops crossed the borders in June 1941, Himmler addressed recruits for Kampfgruppe *Nord* in a speech which is worth quoting at length for the light it sheds on the SS way of thinking.

'For years, for over a decade we old National Socialists have struggled in Germany with Bolshevism. One thing we can be certain of today; what we predicted in our political battle was not exaggerated by one single word or sentence. On the contrary, it was too mild and too weak because we did not, at that time, yet have the insight we have today. It is a great heavenly blessing that, for the first time in a thousand years, fate has given us this Führer. It is a stroke of fate that the Führer, in his turn, decided at the right moment to upset Russia's plans and thus prevent a Russian attack.

'This is an ideological battle and a struggle of races. Here in this struggle stands National Socialism; an ideology based on the value of our Germanic, Nordic blood. Here stands a world as we have conceived it; beautiful, decent, socially equal, that perhaps, in a few instances, is still burdened by shortcomings, but as a whole a happy, beautiful world full of culture; this is what our Germany is like.

'On the other side stands a population of 180 million, a mixture of races whose very names are unpronounceable and whose physique is such that one can shoot them down without pity or compassion. These animals, that torture and ill-treat every prisoner from our side, every wounded man that they come across and do not treat them the way decent soldiers would, you will see for yourself. These people have been welded by the Jews into one religion, one ideology, that is called Bolshevism, with the task; now we have Russia, half of Asia, a part of Europe, now we will overwhelm Germany and the whole world.'

Unfortunately, although some men probably sniggered to themselves, the majority seem to have accepted without demur this style of rhetoric for all its blend of fanaticism and historical and racial distortion. There is, for example, no evidence that Stalin planned an attack on Germany (despite claims by the Soviet intelligence defector 'Victor Suvorov'). Moreover, Jews in Russia were treated in much the same way as in Germany, and hardly masterminded the Russian Revolution! Claims about the mistreatment of prisoners, particularly members of the SS, are true but beg the fact that the SS was doing exactly the same in return. Regardless of the dividing line between insanity and reality though, the German armed forces would learn to their cost that these Russian 'subhumans' (*Untermenschen*) were a foe to be reckoned with. Before then, however, the Army and Waffen-SS had another task to tackle.

*   *   *

To cut a complicated story as short as possible, in April 1939 Italy had invaded Albania and at the end of October 1940 had used this as the springboard from which to attack Greece on a manufactured pretext. Earlier in the same month German troops had marched into Romania, ostensibly to help Marshal Ion Antonescu's government to maintain law and order but actually to safeguard the Ploesti oilfields which were essential to Germany's war effort. World attention thus briefly became focused on the Balkans.

Hitler had repeatedly advised Mussolini to leave Greece alone because an invasion would be bound to draw Britain into the battle and 'his' oilfields would then be vulnerable to attacks by the Royal Air Force. Moreover, so far the Italian army had made a poor showing, and the German dictator feared for its chances against the small but tough Greek army. His forebodings were rapidly proved correct! By the third week in November the Greeks had halted the Italian advance and gone over to the offensive themselves, drawing troops away from their Bulgarian frontier to do so. (At this time Bulgaria was still neutral but, like Yugoslavia, was under steadily increasing pressure to join the Tripartite Alliance between Germany, Italy and Japan.) British troops had also begun arriving, although so far in only small numbers.

An Italian defeat in Greece, coming on top of their reverses in North Africa (where General Sir Archibald Wavell's troops were sweeping them back with heavy losses), would have been a major propaganda disaster for the Axis. On a more pragmatic level, a strong British presence in Greece would have posed a threat to Germany's southern flank when the invasion of Russia commenced. In the middle of December, therefore, Hitler issued a Directive ordering the OKW to start planning for German military intervention in Greece (codenamed Operation 'Marita') and started putting further pressure on the Bulgarian government to allow passage of German troops through their country. By the end of January 1941 Bulgaria had agreed to join the Axis and the Greeks, whose progress against the Italians had been slowed by the winter weather, began looking anxiously over their shoulders.

Yugoslavia was still holding out against joining Hungary, Romania and Bulgaria as a German satellite, but in the middle of March Hitler issued an ultimatum to Prince Paul because he needed to know exactly where he stood when German forces invaded Greece on 6 April. On 25 March Yugoslavia signed a pact with Germany, but during the following night a *coup d'état* overthrew the government and the new leaders repudiated the agreement. Hitler was incensed and ordered that Yugoslavia should be invaded on the same day as Greece, giving the operation the codename *Strafe* ('Punishment'). SS Division *Reich* would take part in this as a component in General Georg-Hans Reinhardt's XLI Panzer Korps while the Leibstandarte *Adolf Hitler* would accompany General Georg Stumme's

XL Panzer Korps in the invasion of Greece.

The weak and poorly equipped Yugoslav army was only able to put up token resistance against the Wehrmacht and Waffen-SS, and the main hindrance to the German plans was the weather which reduced the roads to muddy cart tracks, making swift movement all but impossible. The SS *Reich* Division's reconnaissance battalion, led by Hauptsturmführer Fritz Klingenberg, distinguished itself by capturing Belgrade itself. After a nightmare of a forced march, the unit reached the Danube on 11 April only to find it so swollen by floodwater that a crossing seemed impossible because none of the bridges remained intact. Undeterred, Klingenberg found an old fishing boat and with only 10 volunteers to accompany him, forced a passage. They discovered the Yugoslav capital virtually deserted apart from work parties clearing up the rubble left by the Luftwaffe, and were practically ignored as they marched through the ancient streets. At the German Mission they cleared away an angry crowd and summoned the city's Mayor. Klingenberg issued an ultimatum: surrender, or he would call up a Stuka strike. It was pure bluff because Klingenberg did not even have a radio, but the city was delivered into his hands, together with a thousand prisoners. The news was not believed back at divisional headquarters until a cyclist struggled through with the written proof! Then the champagne bottles were cracked and Klingenberg was awarded the Knights Cross. Yugoslavia formally surrendered on 17 April, by which time Allied forces were also in full retreat in Greece.

Here, the Leibstandarte had encountered rather stiffer opposition. Advancing alongside the 9th Panzer Division, they captured the

Hauptsturmführer Fritz Klingenberg photographed shortly after his audacious capture of Belgrade.

Above *Following the fall of the city, utility cars of the* Reich *Division drive through Belgrade.*

Below *Men of the Leibstandarte in Greece. The solar topees proved unpopular and were soon discarded!*

stronghold of Monastir on the third day of the campaign. They ran into greater difficulties forcing a passage of the Klidi Pass, which was defended by Australians and New Zealanders, and suffered 200 casualties. (There were only 200 German casualties *in total* during the invasion of Yugoslavia!) Then, on the approach to the deep defile of the Klissura Pass, the brigade's reconnaissance battalion found the Greek defenders dug in in well-protected machine-gun nests. The attack faltered as the men flung themselves into shelter from the withering fire. This, decided Kurt 'Panzer' Meyer, the unit commander, was not good enough. The reputation of the Leibstandarte was at stake. Unclipping a grenade from his belt, he pulled the pin and rolled it at his men's heels. 'Never again,' he said later, 'did I witness such a concerted leap forward as at that second!' The pass was captured and, like Klingenberg, Meyer was also awarded the Knights Cross.

After this the Greeks became increasingly disheartened and following the fall of Salonika to other German units advancing along the coast, whole divisions began surrendering in droves. The Greek government surrendered on 22 April and British Empire forces conducted a skilful rearguard action as they retreated into the Peloponessus, from where they were evacuated by sea to Egypt and Crete over the 28/29 April. With his southern flank secured and General Erwin Rommel's newly arrived troops rapidly reversing Wavell's earlier successes in North Africa, Hitler could return his attention to Russia. But a vital month had been lost and the campaign, originally scheduled to begin on 15 May, could not now start until June. This was to have dire consequences later in the year.

*   *   *

Shortly after 03:00 on the morning of 22 June 1941 the thousand-mile Russian frontier from the Baltic to the Black Sea erupted in flame as a massive artillery barrage heralded the beginning of Operation 'Barbarossa' and German tanks and half-tracks began pouring eastwards. Overhead, wave after wave of bombers headed for the Russian airfields, their principal task to destroy the Soviet Air Force on the ground. It was an operation on a scale unprecedented in history. Something between 128 and 154 divisions*, or about 2.5–3 million men in any case, were thrown into the attack, accompanied by 3,330 tanks and 2,770 aircraft. Facing them was an army totalling some twelve million men with 20,000 tanks and 8,000 aircraft, but of the Red Army's 230 divisions, only about 130 were deployed in the path of the Wehrmacht so the odds were not as uneven as appears at first sight. Moreover, the Germans had several other factors riding in their favour and the OKW confidently predicted a successful conclusion to the campaign in eight to 10 weeks.

* The number varies widely according to source and reflects the ambiguous position of some reserve, security and foreign formations and the dates they actually began moving forward. Even such respected and widely quoted authorities as Field Marshal Erich Manstein and General Heinz Guderian fail to make their figures match.

Waffen-SS troops step on to Russian soil past a frontier marker post.

Ever paranoid, in 1937 Stalin had unleashed his dreaded secret police, the NKVD, on the army, and thousands of his most able senior officers were executed in what has become known as the 'Tukachevsky Purge', Marshal Mikhail Tukachevsky being the most prominent officer killed. The loss of these men left the Red Army with few capable commanders at either staff or field level, while by comparison the German Army was the best led in the world. The Red Army had already been given a bloody nose by tiny Finland in the Winter War of 1940–1, and there had not been time to rectify its shortcomings in the few intervening months. Most of its tanks and aircraft were obsolescent, although the new T–34 just entering production would come as a nasty shock to the *Panzertruppen*. Moreover, few Russian tanks had radios, and company commanders had to semaphore their intentions to the other vehicles under command by standing in the turret waving a pair of flags! On top of this, such was Stalin's distrust of the Army that each unit had an NKVD officer attached as a political commissar, which did not help troop morale. (See also Commissar Order below.)

German morale, on the other hand, was generally high after nearly two years of nothing but victories, although a few officers did express the view that this time Hitler had bitten off more than he could chew. (Many other officers did so subsequently, proving how accurate hindsight is...) The nucleus of the attacking forces were troops who had proved their mettle on several battlefields, had learned to work together, had faith in their equipment and their leadership, and were not superstitiously deterred by the fact that the date chosen for the beginning of the campaign was the anniversary of Napoleon crossing the River Niemen in 1812. High morale certainly prevailed among the Waffen-SS units, and although numerically a mere drop in the bucket of German might, they were soon to prove their worth.

The Leibstandarte *Adolf Hitler* had been rapidly expanded to the size of a full motorized division between April and June and had been numbered first in the roll–call of SS formations. The Waffen-SS divisions had been allocated as follows in the line-up for Operation 'Barbarossa' (the foregoing

Left *Men of the* Reich *Division march across the seemingly endless steppe.*

Below Totenkopf *troops in a Krupp 6 × 4 L2H43 light truck towing a 3.7 cm PaK 35/36 across a stream. This little anti-tank gun was already obsolescent and of no value against the Soviet T-34 tank.*

remarks about exact numbers should be borne in mind).

1st SS-Division (mot) Leibstandarte *Adolf Hitler*: with General Ewald von Kleist's 1st Panzergruppe as part of Field Marshal Gerd von Rundstedt's Army Group South (5 Panzer, 3–4 motorized, 21–22 infantry, 6 mountain or *jäger* (light) and 3 security divisions plus 14–15 Romanian, 2 Hungarian and 2 Italian divisions).

2nd SS-Division (mot) *Reich*: with General Heinz Guderian's 2nd Panzergruppe as part of Field Marshal Fedor von Bock's Army Group Centre (9 Panzer, 5 motorized and 31–35 infantry divisions as well as 2–3 security divisions, a cavalry division and the *Großdeutschland* Regiment).

3rd SS-Division (mot) *Totenkopf*: with General Erich Höppner's 4th Panzergruppe as part of Field Marshal Ritter von Leeb's Army Group North (the weakest of the Army Groups with only 3 Panzer, 3 motorized and some 20 infantry divisions).

4th SS Polizei Division: in reserve with Army Group North.

5th SS-Division (mot) *Wiking*: with Kleist's Panzergruppe in Army Group South.

Kampfgruppe *Nord*, together with the 9th SS Infantry Standarte from Norway, would be withdrawn from the line to be brought up to divisional strength and trained as a *Gebirgsjäger* (mountain troop) unit after their dismal performance during the early days of the campaign, when they were assigned to the Finnish Front (Finland having allied itself to Germany for the attack on Russia alone, and not getting involved in the war elsewhere).

Perhaps surprisingly, *Wiking* was the strongest of the SS divisions with 19,377 men; *Reich* was second with 19,021, *Totenkopf* third with 18,754, the Polizei Division fourth with 17,347, the Leibstandarte (still being brought up to strength) fifth with 10,796 and *Nord* sixth with 10,573 (figures courtesy George H. Stein extracted from a report to Himmler dated 27 August 1941).

The initial objectives of the campaign were clear: Army Group North was to advance through the Baltic states of Latvia, Lithuania and Estonia (which had been annexed by Russia in 1940) and in conjunction with Finnish and German troops moving down from the north capture Leningrad; Army Group Centre was to capture Moscow; and Army Group South was to capture Kiev, Kharkov and the Crimea prior to driving on to the River Volga, the psychologically important city of Stalingrad and the even more important oilfields surrounding the Caucasus Mountains. Of still greater importance than the territorial objectives, though, was the destruction of the Red Army in the field. It was an over-ambitious plan in the first place, despite all the revisions it went through, and it is a miracle that the Wehrmacht so nearly succeeded, especially in view of modifications that were introduced while the campaign was in progress.

To begin with, the offensive went almost better than the OKW could have dared to hope. The Russians were taken completely by surprise (something which has always baffled historians because Stalin had plenty of forewarning, even if German troop movements towards their start lines were disguised as redeployments of reserves). German signallers intercepted frantic radio messages from Russian units saying they were being attacked, and asking what should they do? Replies to these signals cast doubts upon the senders' sanity!

Army Group South encountered the stiffest resistance because they faced the strongest opposition, in particular from six mechanized corps under the very capable General Mikhail Kirponos. From its start line near Lublin in Poland the Leibstandarte nevertheless headed rapidly towards the River Vistula, aiming for Galicia and the western Ukraine. The first check came at Romanovka when the division first encountered the Russian T–34 tank; Rupert Butler (see *Further reading*) provides a graphic description of the scene.

> 'Here was something that could not be kicked, whipped, bullied or machine-gunned. This magnificent piece of armour was immune except to the 88 mm flak gun. The Soviets came in continuous waves against the thin SS formations…
>
> 'The attacks came hourly and the men of the Leibstandarte noticed that the troops seemed to be of an altogether higher calibre, at least in terms of violent courage, than the Germans had encountered previously. Charges were made with the bayonet and engagements were hand-to-hand. In country of deep forest, Germans and Russians hacked and stabbed at one another, while mortars burst their lethal shrapnel.'

Only after Luftwaffe support was summoned did the Soviet onslaught diminish and the Leibstandarte become capable of pressing on towards Kiev.

Meanwhile *Wiking* moved forward decisively from its own start point at Cholm through Lemberg and Tarnopol and had reached Zhitomir by the time the Leibstandarte was fighting the above battle in mid-July. It pressed on to Byela Tserkov Usin by the end of the month and then assisted the Leibstandarte in closing the Uman pocket. The favourite, and most successful, German tactic on the Eastern Front was to send the Panzer and motorized divisions in sweeping encircling movements deep into the Russian lines, closing in two pincers around dozens of Soviet divisions to trap them and cut them off from their lines of communication and supply while the slower-moving infantry divisions applied pressure from the west. Hundreds of thousands of Russian soldiers were netted in this way and found their way into captivity. Unfortunately, early successes of this nature caused Hitler to make a major change in his operational orders in mid-July, and this was to have a significant effect on the whole course of the campaign.

Reich *Division SdKfz 221 armoured car. In the German armed forces, most vehicles were assigned a* Sonderkraftfahrzeug *or special purpose vehicle number.*

The 2nd SS-Division *Reich*, reinforced by a battalion of *Sturmgeschütz* (StuG) III assault guns, was grouped with the 10th Panzer Division and elements of the *Großdeutschland* as part of a reserve corps in Guderian's 2nd Panzergruppe, and did not get into action until four days after the start of the campaign, once tanks equipped with schnorkels had forced a crossing of the River Bug. Thereafter, though, the division was in the thick of things, forcing a bridgehead over the River Beresina and providing flank guard for the speeding Panzers as they headed on towards the Dnieper and the first major objective, Smolensk. They reached Gorki in mid-July and the 2nd Panzergruppe completed a major encirclement around Yelnya while General Hermann Hoth's 3rd Panzergruppe achieved a similar objective further east around Smolensk. The prize was 300,000 prisoners and 3,000 tanks captured or destroyed to add to the similar numbers already achieved. Not satisfied with this, Guderian and Hoth completed similar encirclements around Gomel and Roslavl by the 24th which produced another 120,000 prisoners.

It was these successes which prompted Hitler's fatal change of mind referred to above. Temporarily abandoning Moscow as an objective, he assigned Army Group Centre's two Panzergruppen new tasks: Guderian's force was to swing southwards to help von Kleist in a mammoth encirclement around Kiev while Hoth's would go north to assist Höppner. *Reich*, however, was left behind guarding the left flank of the Yelnya salient. It held out for a fortnight against a Russian force of 11 divisions (two of them armoured) before being withdrawn with heavy casualties to

Left *A dapper SS officer with Knights Cross at his throat alongside another SdKfz 221. This vehicle was normally just armed with a 7.92 mm machine-gun but variants mounted a 2 or 2.8 cm light cannon.*

Below *Victorious SS troops with a captured Russian flag.*

recuperate, but was back in the fray by the beginning of September.

In Army Group North's sector the advance had been less spectacular because the sandy, heavily forested terrain favoured the defenders, but after a major battle against two Soviet armoured corps, von Leeb's troops were in Daugavpils (Dvinsk) where the bridge had been captured by a daring advance party of the elite *Brandenburg* commando regiment. After a pause to let the slower-moving infantry catch up, Höppner's Panzergruppe (General Erich Manstein's LVI and Georg-Hans Reinhardt's XVI Panzer Korps) pushed on in the general direction of Lake Ilmen against stiffening opposition. Around Noroshev, Manstein ran headlong into another Soviet armoured corps and his advance was checked in the swamps and woods. He separated his three divisions, *Totenkopf* bypassing the obstacle to the south and breaking through the so-called Stalin Line* around Opochka, while Reinhardt's Korps was forcing a breakthrough at Pskov, on the southern shore of Lake Peipus. Pushing on towards Novgorod, at one stage in the middle of July Manstein's Korps was surrounded and unable to break out for three days, a foretaste of things to come.

Höppner's two Korps pushed on into Estonia regardless, but in the third week of July Hitler, alarmed at the way in which the armoured and motorized units had outstripped the infantry (including the Polizei Division, which had yet to see any action), ordered a halt until Hoth's Panzergruppe could be sent to help. This caused a disastrous three-week delay which gave the citizens of Leningrad time to build up the city's fortifications. Meanwhile, on the Finnish front progress had been slow and Kampfgruppe *Nord* had disgraced the Waffen-SS by panicking and running away at the battle of Salla; the survivors were taken out of the line and sent to Austria for retraining. Brought up to strength as a full alpine division, *Nord* did not return to the front until August, 1942, rechristened 6th SS-Gebirgs (Mountain) Division *Nord*.

Himmler and Gottlob Berger had been busy during the summer raising yet more Waffen-SS formations. Four *Totenkopf* Standarten which had been serving in a security role in the occupied countries were brought together in Poland, kitted out as infantry and formed into two unnamed brigades, while the fifth remaining Standarte became SS Infantry Regiment No 5. The *Totenkopf* organization also had two cavalry Standarten and these were similarly brought together as the SS-Kavallerie Brigade. Later, in the summer of 1942, this would be increased to the size of a division and given the name 8th SS-Kavallerie Division *Florian Geyer*. In the meantime, however, the brigade was used in the anti-partisan role behind the front line in Russia, where it acquired a definitely unsavoury reputation.

Partisan units had begun springing up within days of the German invasion. Russian soldiers who had escaped the battles of encirclement but become separated from their units banded themselves together in the forests and swamps. Initially their efforts at disrupting the German rear

---

* Not so much a real line as a staggered series of fortified points which could easily be bypassed by mobile formations.

areas by attacking isolated outposts or supply convoys were very much on an ad hoc basis, but the Soviet high command, STAVKA, soon came to appreciate their value and a new department was set up to co-ordinate their efforts while paratroops were dropped in to reinforce them, bringing radios, arms and ammunition in the same way as the British Special Operations Executive (SOE) and American Office of Strategic Services (OSS) assisted the resistance forces in the other occupied countries. In Russia, the partisans rapidly became a menace to the Germans rather than a mere nuisance, and extreme measures were taken to stamp them out. In this, the SS played a major role.

Being principally an ideological war against a foe whom German soldiers had been indoctrinated into believing 'subhuman', the campaign in the east was conducted by both sides with unparallelled savagery. Prisoners were frequently executed out of hand by front line troops, while in the rear areas practically no one was safe. The irony is that Hitler's racial policies created enemies out of many potential allies. In the Baltic states which had so recently been overrun by Russia, and in the fiercely independent Ukraine, the German troops were originally welcomed as liberators, festooned with flowers and cheered as they drove through towns and villages. The euphoria soon ceased when the extermination squads began arriving in the wake of the real soldiers.

Four *Einsatzgruppen* had originally been created by Heydrich under the overall leadership of SD Brigadeführer Professor Otto Ohlendorf for

Men of the Polizei Division with dogs to track down partisans.

An SS officer (whether of an Einsatzgruppe *or not is unknown) administers the* coupe de grâce *to suspected partisans executed by firing squad.*

'security' duties in Poland. Designated A, B, C and D, each consisted of between 500 and 1,000 men and they were to be responsible for the murder of over a million Russian Jews in the first year of the campaign alone. Giving testimony at Nürnberg, Ohlendorf described a typical operation.

> 'The unit selected for this task would enter a village or city and order the prominent Jewish citizens to call together all Jews for the purpose of resettlement. They were requested to hand over their valuables to the leaders of the unit and shortly before the execution to surrender their outer clothing. The men, women and children were led to a place of execution which in most cases was located next to a more deeply excavated anti-tank ditch. Then they were shot kneeling or standing, and the corpses thrown into the ditch.'

The calm, unapologetic manner in which Ohlendorf answered all the questions thrown at him did not alter the Nürnberg verdict, and he was hanged in 1951. Many other men could not, after a time, stand the slaughter though and requested transfers; even Himmler was sickened when he witnessed one of these executions. Approximately 3,000 men in total served in the *Einsatzgruppen*. They were not part of the Waffen-SS but part of the SD. Nevertheless, as with the concentration camps, there *was* an interchange of personnel and Waffen-SS units were frequently

Latvian members of the Waffen-SS in action.

commandeered to assist in the murders — but so were regular Army troops as well.

Nor were Jews the only victims of the *Einsatzgruppen*. Hitler had ordered that all Commissars and members of the Russian secret police should be executed the moment they were identified. (This order was issued to the Army as well as the SS but many unit commanders up to and including

Field Marshals refused to implement it.) Then, as the partisan movement gathered momentum, tens of thousands more people were swept up in the action groups' nets, many of them completely innocent, and it was this which caused a wave of revulsion to replace the local support given earlier to the front line troops. Nevertheless, the energetic Gottlob Berger still succeeded in recruiting tens of thousands of anti-Communist and anti-Semitic volunteers into new formations to swell the ranks of the Waffen-SS.

In Latvia the first volunteers began joining internal security battalions to assist the *Einsatzgruppen* and Gestapo as early as July 1941. Later, in early 1943 some of these were grouped together into the Lettische SS-Freiwilligen Legion (Latvian SS-Volunteer Legion) and issued with SS-pattern uniforms, although like all the foreign volunteer units they had their own distinctive collar patch insignia. Later in the year the Legion was increased to the size of a Brigade and in early 1944 it became the 15th Waffen Grenadier Division der SS (lettische Nr 1). A second Latvian division was raised at the same time from other security battalions, becoming the 19th Waffen Grenadier Division der SS (lettische Nr 2). Both fought in the northern sector for the remainder of the war until finally surrendering in East Prussia in 1945. The 15th Division proved the toughest and most reliable of the eastern volunteer formations in the Waffen-SS.

Meanwhile, in March/April 1943 two further divisions were raised, one in Estonia and one in the Ukraine (where an incredible 30,000 volunteers attempted to enrol). These became the 14th and 20th Waffen Grenadier Divisionen der SS (galizische Nr 1 and estnische Nr 1); the title of the former was later changed to ukrainische Nr 1. Both divisions fought well, the Ukrainians especially so since they knew their fate would be unpleasant to say the least if they were captured by the Russians. The Estonian Division retreated into Prussia and Silesia where they surrendered alongside the Latvians in May 1945. The Ukrainian Division was all but wiped out in July 1944 and was never re-formed although some survivors carried on fighting from secret hideouts in the Carpathian Mountains until 1946; the remainder surrendered into British custody at the end of the war and counted themselves lucky not to be repatriated.

Ukrainian volunteers from prisoner-of-war camps also made up the bulk of the 6,500 men in the brigade-sized 29th Waffen Grenadier Division der SS (russische Nr 1) which was formed in 1943 under the leadership of a particularly unsavoury character called Bratislav Kaminsky. The 'Kaminsky Brigade', as it became generally known, was responsible for many behind-the-lines atrocities, including the murder of an estimated 10,000 Poles during the Warsaw Uprising in August 1944. The Brigade's behaviour shocked and nauseated even other hardened SS men and Erich von dem Bach-Zelewski (a former *Einsatzgruppe* commander), who was in charge of the Warsaw operation, claimed at Nürnberg that he had Kaminsky executed; certainly he disappeared and his body was never found. The

Left *A Ukrainian housewife pours a glass of milk for an SS trooper from the* Westland *Standarte.*

Below *Soviet cossacks in German service. The vehicle is a StuG III assault gun with 7.5 cm main armament.*

Brigade was then broken up, some men going to the so-called Russian Liberation Army formed in 1944 by Lieutenant-General Andrei Vlasov* and the remainder to the 30th Waffen Grenadier Division der SS (russische Nr 2). This in itself had been formed from renegade Russian security troops in July/August 1944 and assigned to anti-*Maquis* (Resistance) duties in France, but it was disbanded in November the same year and its personnel distributed amongst other SS divisions and Vlasov's units.

*   *   *

Returning now to operations on the Eastern Front in the autumn of 1941, in the north *Totenkopf* and the Polizei Division† were more or less left on their own with a collection of Army infantry divisions in II Korps to complete the investment of Leningrad, while Höppner's 4th Panzergruppe was diverted southwards to assist in Army Group Centre's hoped-for final assault on Moscow which had been so delayed by the operations around Kiev. For each of the front line divisions it was to be a winter of trial, perhaps for *Totenkopf* most of all. During October the Germans tightened their ring around Leningrad but the earlier delays had given the city's inhabitants, spurred on by Marshal Georgi Zhukov, time to dig and build formidable defences through which the infantry were unable to penetrate. By the middle of November all attempts to advance any further were halted by the weather and the troops could do nothing but dig in and shiver. (The men of the Waffen-SS were more fortunate than their Army colleagues in this respect, for the SS commissariat had had the foresight to order protective winter parkas, overtrousers, boots and mittens while the Army provided no more than the standard greatcoat and thin woollen gloves. Huge numbers of fur coats, hats and padded boots were therefore requisitioned from the local population, and the vaunted Wehrmacht began to look more like a collection of refugees from a jumble sale than the Army which had conquered almost all of Europe.)

The *Totenkopf* Division dug itself into the natural defensive position of the Valdai Hills during December, a period when Russian activity was ominously quiet on their front. Then, when Zhukov — who had been transferred from Leningrad to take over the defence of Moscow — launched the second phase of his winter counter-offensive in the middle of a blizzard during the night of 7/8 January 1942, it was *Totenkopf* which bore its brunt.

---

* Vlasov was dedicated to the overthrow of Stalin. Captured in 1942, he readily threw in his lot with the Germans and made numerous propaganda speeches on the radio. His Army was two divisions strong and included large numbers of Cossacks. At the end of the war he was recaptured by Soviet troops and executed for treason in 1946. Most of his men who had fallen into American or British hands were forcibly repatriated, many of them committing suicide when they realized they were being sent back to Russia — an unpleasant episode in Western history.

† Which was still not formally a part of the Waffen-SS even though its members wore the SS sleeve eagle; it would become a 'proper' Waffen-SS unit in February 1942.

Top *SS troops in the autumn of 1941.*

Above *As weather conditions deteriorated, the troops found that normal winter issue clothing was inadequate in Russia.*

(The first phase during December had been directed against Army Group Centre, as described later; the second phase was designed to drive a wedge between Army Groups North and Centre and very nearly succeeded.) The two Army divisions either side of *Totenkopf* were thrown back in disorder with heavy casualties, leaving the line held almost solely by Eicke's so often maligned troops. They had already suffered heavily over the previous months, losing nearly 9,000 men dead or wounded, roughly 50 per cent of their strength, while replacements only totalled half this number.

Five of the division's battalions had to be rushed to the important rail and road junction of Staraya Russa and two more to Demyansk in order to stem the Soviet advance, and the commander of Army Group North, Field Marshal Ritter Wilhelm von Leeb, resigned when Hitler refused to give permission for II Korps to retire to prepared positions behind the River Lovat. By 20 January the *Totenkopf* and other isolated units of the Korps were completely cut off except at Staraya Russa, where they managed to establish a 'breakwater'. Three weeks later the Russians had surrounded all of six divisions, including *Totenkopf*, in the area around Demyansk. Such was the SS troops' fighting quality that when the situation clarified on 8 February they were split into two battlegroups which included Army personnel. They were to act as the 'fire brigade' within the pocket, to stem any Russian incursion (a role to which the premier Waffen-SS divisions were to become accustomed). The situation was so critical that Eicke had to order all his walking wounded back into the line from the field hospitals. Mere companies, sometimes of only 40 or 50 men, had to repulse assaults on a divisional scale — and succeeded. The only villages the Russians recaptured were those in which every *Totenkopf* soldier had been killed.

By the end of February only isolated groups of soldiers still fought on, separated by the arctic wilderness and the enemy from their comrades. The Russians persisted despite hideous casualties in mounting frontal assaults First World War–style, their infantry charging forward with fixed bayonets into the teeth of the German machine-gun, mortar and artillery fire, and dying in droves. But the defenders in the Demyansk pocket were in a desperate situation. They could no longer evacuate their seriously wounded and the Luftwaffe had to parachute in their supplies, ammunition being the first priority. A mere 400 replacements were flown in early in March. Still they held on. Then, in the second week of March, the weather began improving and the supply situation with it. An attempt to relieve the survivors in the pocket could now be planned and X Korps was assembled behind the Lovat to strike towards them from the direction of Staraya Russa.

Supported by the greatest concentration of aircraft seen over the northern front all winter, the attack began on 22 March but was brought to a halt six days later. Clearing a path through the Russians took another fortnight and it was not until 14 April, with spring in the air, that Eicke's emaciated command was able to strike westwards to effect a link-up. On 22 April, after 73 days of isolation, the *Totenkopf* Division re-established contact with the outside world. Shortly afterwards it was withdrawn from the line and sent back for a rest and refit in France. It would return to the fray in February 1943, re-equipped as a fully fledged Panzergrenadier division with an integral battalion of tanks.

Meanwhile, on Army Group Centre's front, *Reich* had been having a far from easy time. At the end of September it was attached, along with the Army's crack *Großdeutschland* Regiment and XLVI Panzer Korps, to Höppner's 4th Panzergruppe when it moved down from the northern

StuG IIIs of the Totenkopf *Division in the early spring of 1942 after their ordeal in the Demyansk pocket.*

front. Now it was to take part in Operation *Taifun* ('Typhoon'), the assault on Moscow. This began officially on 2 October although Guderian's 2nd Panzergruppe had set off a couple of days earlier because he was, wisely, worried about the state of the roads which were rapidly disintegrating in the torrential rain. Nevertheless, to begin with the attack seemed to be going well. On 6 October *Reich* was entrusted with the task of cutting the Smolensk-Moscow highway between Gzhansk and Vyazma, completing an encirclement around the latter town. They reached this position after three days despite tough opposition, including continuous strafing by Russian fighters, but on 9 October the weather broke and the men moved out into the teeth of a raging blizzard. Nevertheless they took Gzhansk, and two days later were hurled against the defenders in front of Mozhaisk, who had artillery support from an armoured train. Despite their suicidal courage, the Russians found their lines broken at several places and had to retreat with *Reich* in hot pursuit. The *Der Führer* Regiment captured the historic battlefield of Borodino* on 15 October and three days later the division broke into Mozhaisk itself, supported by the 10th Panzer Division which was fiercely engaged by Soviet T–34s in several furious encounters which the *Panzertruppen* generally succeeded in winning due to their far

---

* Scene of the major clash between the Russians and Napoleon's *Grande Armée* during the French advance on Moscow in 1812.

superior training, tactics and communications. (The Waffen-SS divisions at this stage had few tanks of their own apart largely from captured ones repainted with prominent white or black and white crosses to replace the red stars.)

At this moment victory seemed in the air. 'Prisoners,' recalled General Günther Blumentritt, the Fourth Army Chief of Staff (who in 1944 would be given the SS rank of Obergruppenführer and appointed to command of XII SS Korps), 'prisoners told us that this new attack, launched so late in the year, had been completely unexpected. Moscow seemed about to fall into our hands.' So still the Germans advanced, despite 15 or more degrees of frost and the arrival of tough winter-trained Russian reinforcements from Siberia and Mongolia, but by the third week in November it was clear that the optimism had been unjustified. *Reich* had shot its bolt with Moscow a tantalizing 18 miles away. The division had helped enormously in the capture of 600,000 Russian troops in the Vyazma and Bryansk pockets but had lost some 7,000 of its own men since the beginning of Operation *Taifun* and the survivors were totally exhausted while the Russians, whom everyone had thought were on the run, seemed to have inexhaustible reserves.

It was at this point, when the German divisions were at the end of their

The man on the left has a purloined sheepskin coat underneath his camouflage smock, while on the right a motor cycle rider keeps warm in the standard double-breasted rubberized coat with leather helmet and goggles.

tether, that Marshal Zhukov launched the first phase of his own winter counter-offensive. He had assembled two new 'Shock Armies' for this whose aim was to split Field Marshal Günther von Kluge's Fourth Army away from its armoured support by driving wedges between it and the 3rd and 4th Panzergruppen on its northern flank and the 2nd on its southern.

Hitler had ordered 'no retreat' for neither the first nor the last time, a command which many of his Generals and Field Marshals considered insane but which in fact can be seen in retrospect as the correct decision, because the appalling weather conditions would have permitted a retreat of perhaps only three miles under the cover of one of the long nights. (The sun did not emerge from the mist until after nine in the morning and set by three in the afternoon.) A proper strategic withdrawal would have required much greater mobility than these conditions allowed. Lubricating oil froze solid in the vehicles' engines unless they were kept warmed, fires had to be lit beneath tanks to keep their water cooling systems liquefied, gun breeches sealed themselves closed, ungloved fingers were welded by cold to any metal surface, frostbite caused more casualties than enemy bullets and any sentry who had the misfortune to fall asleep chanced

White sheets were used as improvised snow camouflage until proper reversible grey/white snow suits were issued.

Men of the Reich *Division huddle round a fire for warmth.*

literally freezing to death where he stood. *This* was the reality of the Russian Front in winter.

Instead of withdrawing, therefore, the Germans established defensive 'hedgehogs' with well dug-in positions and entrenched artillery. Troops in the front line, where a 'line' existed at all, could retire into these to allow the Soviet armour to expend itself fruitlessly in the bleak countryside, like cavalry in Napoleon's day sweeping around the outthrust bayonets of infantry squares. The Germans' problems were exacerbated by partisan attacks on their supply convoys and Zhukov's use of paratroops, ski troops and Cossacks in deep forays behind the lines, but the standard form of Russian infantry attack remained the suicidal frontal charge and this caused so many casualties that a week into his counter-attack Zhukov had to issue a specific order for them to cease.

The Russian offensive began by making good headway. On 8 December — at the same time that, in a different time zone on the other side of the world, Japanese bombers were pounding Pearl Harbor — Guderian's 2nd Panzergruppe was being forced back from Tula to avoid the encirclement threatened by the retreat of Thirteenth Army on its flank. A fortnight later Hitler sacked Guderian, a fate which would befall several other senior officers who ignored or argued against the 'no retreat' order. To the north, Kluge's Fourth Army, including *Reich*, was also in a bad way. General

An SS Feldgendarmerie *or military police detachment outside their bunker on the outskirts of a Russian town. The gorgets they wore gave them the nickname 'chained dogs'.*

Blumentritt says that, having obtained his first objective in forcing Guderian back, Zhukov then split his forces, some heading towards Kaluga, others advancing in the Oka sector and still more in the direction of Maloyaroslavets. 'Russian intentions were obvious,' he later wrote. 'They were planning a wide double encirclement... by means of attacks both in the north and the south, with the ultimate aim of surrounding and destroying [Fourth Army] in its present positions west of Moscow.' The Germans had no reserves and only one road still lay open towards the west.

By Christmas Eve Fourth Army's situation was desperate. All that lay between headquarters in Maloyaroslavets and the 'Red tide' were 50 surviving tanks of the 19th Panzer Division, while some of the other Panzer divisions were down to no more than a dozen or so tanks in running order. The German positions seemed doomed, but now it was the Russians' turn to run out of steam and this proved the salvation of Army Group Centre, since Zhukov transferred his attention to the northern sector where he had fresh troops, as we have seen. *Reich* badly needed the reprieve for they had lost heavily in the winter fighting — some 4,000 men up to mid-February — and like *Totenkopf* they were taken out of the line and sent back to France to recuperate and be re-equipped as a Panzergrenadier division with the revised title *Das Reich*. (A few of the fitter survivors remained in Russia as a 'battlegroup'; others took part in the vain attempt to prevent the French scuttling their fleet at Toulon when the Allies invaded Morocco and Algeria in November 1942; but effectively the division was out of the war until the beginning of 1943.)

What about the Leibstandarte *Adolf Hitler* and *Wiking* during this critical period? After the great encirclement battles around Uman and Kiev, Army Group South headed ever further eastward and it was during this period that the full brutality of the campaign was brought home to 'Sepp' Dietrich's men. In Taganrog they found the bodies of six of their comrades dumped in a well, having been hacked to pieces with axes after being horribly tortured. On their commander's orders, the Leibstandarte took no further prisoners for the next three days.

The Leibstandarte was part of General Eberhard von Mackensen's III Panzer Korps in Ewald von Kleist's 1st Panzergruppe during the advance through the Ukraine and drew unstinting praise from their Korps commander who wrote a unsolicited testimonial to Himmler. He said, 'Its inner discipline, its cool daredeviltry, its cheerful enterprise, its unshakable firmness in a crisis, its exemplary toughness, its camaraderie — all these are outstanding and cannot be surpassed'. Nor was Mackensen alone among Army generals in regarding the Waffen-SS formations as genuine elite units and their approbation led in due course to Hitler's authorization of further expansion and the creation of new German divisions as well as those being created from foreign volunteers.

Army Group South eventually reached Rostov-on-Don and penetrated deeply into the Crimea, although the fortress port of Sevastopol held out for the time being, *Wiking* distinguishing itself in the fierce battle for the important industrial city of Dnepropetrovsk. At Rostov, however, the onslaught faltered, the troops too weary and their tanks and other vehicles too worn out to continue. Then, as in the north and centre, the Russians launched a winter counter-attack which forced the Germans grudgingly

SS officers interrogate a Russian prisoner.

Left *SS sniper with a Kar 98k rifle fitted with telescopic sight.*

Below right *Leon De-grelle with other men of the* Légion Wallonie.

back to defensive positions behind the River Msus. The Soviet attack culminated in a thrust to retake Kharkov in mid-January which left a deep salient into the German lines, but failed to complete its objective due to timely action on the part of Fedor von Bock, who had replaced von Rundstedt as commander of Army Group South. With the situation thus stabilized, the German high command could begin planning their own spring offensive. The Leibstandarte was withdrawn and sent back to France alongside *Reich* and *Totenkopf* to rest and refit as a Panzergrenadier division. *Wiking*, however, was left in the line but would receive reinforcements in May in the shape of the nucleus of the 5th SS Panzer Regiment which would turn it, too, into a Panzergrenadier division.

On 12 May, six days before the Germans had themselves planned to strike, Marshal Semyon Timoshenko renewed his own offensive out of the salient north and south of Kharkov. It was an ill-advised move because the Germans counter-attacked vigorously with First Panzer and Seventeenth Armies from the south and Sixth Army from the north. Timoshenko made the mistake of withholding his reserves until it was too late, and the Germans achieved another mammoth encirclement around Izyum which netted 239,000 prisoners. Despite this success, it caused a month's delay in the start of *Fall Blau* ('Case Blue'), the drive on Stalingrad, the Caucasus Mountains and the priceless Maikop oilfields, a month which would have dire consequences for Sixth Army.

For *Fall Blau* Army Group South was split into two, Army Group A under Field Marshal Siegmund Wilhelm List and Group B under von Bock, the former — including *Wiking* — heading for the Caucasus and the latter towards Stalingrad while Erich von Manstein's Eleventh Army continued mopping up in the Crimea, finally capturing Sevastopol on 3 July. The operation began on 28 June and initially the German Blitzkrieg seemed to be working once more, for the Russians were steadily forced back, but it was a risky operation because of the long northern flank exposed, and made even more so because this was largely held by Hungarian, Italian and Romanian divisions of dubious fighting quality.

One of Germany's friends provided a fighting unit of rather higher calibre during this period. This was Léon Degrelle, leader of the Belgian Rexist Party, which was in almost equal measures nationalistic, anti-Communist and *Roman Catholic*. His movement had been politically unsuccessful pre-war and he had avoided direct collusion with the German occupying forces in 1940, but with the invasion of Russia he had offered to raise a volunteer legion of like-minded compatriots (who were neither necessarily Fascists nor National Socialists) to fight alongside the Germans in their effort to crush Stalin and all he stood for. It is from the writings of men like Degrelle, truthful if misguided and often confusing raconteurs, that the myth of a pre-NATO *European* crusade against Communism emerged. (The total number of Western European volunteers to serve with the German armed forces was 130,000, of whom 50,000 were Dutch, 22,000 Flemish, 20,000 Wallonien, 20,000 French, 6,000 Norwegian, 6,000 Danish, 800 Swiss and 300 Swedish, plus a smattering of other nationalities. Although substantial, these figures obviously only reflect a tiny percentage of the overall population.)

Degrelle's *Légion Wallonie* (Wallonien Legion) was the first foreign volunteer unit to be accepted by the Wehrmacht as opposed to the Waffen-

SS and initially consisted of just 800 men. Degrelle himself served as a mere private to begin with, wishing to share all his men's experiences. Of the original 800 volunteers, only three, including Degrelle, survived the war, but there was a constant flow of replacements and ultimately some 6,000 Walloons fought in the Legion, of whom 2,500 finally survived. (Degrelle, incidentally, was the most highly decorated foreigner in the German armed forces, earning the Knights Cross with Oak Leaves.)

The Legion entrained for the Ukraine in October 1941, fought alongside *Wiking* in the Caucasus region in 1942, returned to Belgium early in 1943 and was increased to the size of a Brigade in June, being incorporated into the SS as the 5th SS-Freiwilligen Sturmbrigade *Wallonien*. It particularly distinguished itself at Cherkassy in January/February 1944, suffering horrendous casualties (see next chapter), and in October the same year was brought up to strength and retitled the 28th SS-Freiwilligen Panzergrenadier Division *Wallonien* with Degrelle as its commander. The unit remained devoutly Catholic throughout, having its own padres and conducting church services regardless of the generally atheistic or agnostic character of the SS as a whole. (Having said that, it should also be stated that within the *German* Waffen-SS divisions, between 30 and 50 per cent remained churchgoers despite all of Himmler's attempts to expunge 'superstition'.)

Later, the *Wallonien* Division took part in the 'Battle of the Bulge' and at the end of the war some of its personnel were captured in Schleswig-Holstein/Denmark, others by the Russians. Degrelle, who considered himself a patriot, not a collaborator, escaped to Spain where Franco gave him sanctuary for a while but in the end he emigrated to Argentina to avoid extradition by the Belgian government. At the time of writing he is still alive, aged 83.

Degrelle's Wallonien Legion was one of seven Western European formations raised after the beginning of the Russian campaign to take part in the fight against Bolshevism; in addition there was a battalion of 400 Finnish volunteers who were given permission by their government to join the Waffen-SS instead of the national army and these were attached to *Wiking*, eventually growing to a strength of 1,180 men before being recalled in June 1943. (Finland signed a unilateral ceasefire agreement with Russia in 1944 and subsequently co-operated with the Red Army in driving out the remaining German troops as a 'guarantee' of a subsequent independence — albeit an uneasy one — from Soviet occupation.)

The second national formation was French and, being 'non-Germanic' like the Walloon contingent, to begin with became part of the Wehrmacht rather than the SS.* In July 1941 the Vichy government introduced

---

* As did the Spanish contingent in Russia, which was never incorporated into the Waffen-SS. Raised in gratitude for the Condor Legion's contribution to victory in the Spanish Civil War, the volunteer 250th Division *Azul* ('Blue Division'), named after the colour of its men's Falangist shirts, fought on the Leningrad front from late 1941 until recalled in 1943 when Franco succumbed to Anglo-American pressure and the realization that, although not yet defeated, Germany could not hope to win the war.

legislation to permit Frenchmen to fight alongside the Germans in Russia and there were sufficient volunteers to fill a regiment within a month — many of them wearing decorations earned in the battle *against* Germany a year previously! The unit entrained for the front as the 638th *Régiment Renforcé d'Infanterie Française* and first saw action west of Moscow in October. It was subsequently renamed *Légion Volontaire Française* then in August 1943 was incorporated into the Waffen-SS as the Französiches SS-Freiwilligen Grenadier Regiment. The Frenchmen fought well and suffered heavy casualties, being withdrawn to Bohemia-Moravia in July 1944 to be reinforced and again renamed, this time as the Französiches Freiwilligen Sturmbrigade *Charlemagne* (the honour title being named after the medieval Emperor). At the beginning of 1945 it was designated the 33rd Waffen Grenadier Division der SS *Charlemagne* (französiches Nr 1) in keeping with what was then the general practice, although like most of the late war formations of this nature it was a 'division' on paper only. A few survivors entered American captivity at the end of the war but the remainder disappeared, either killed or changing into civilian clothing to sink into anonymity and avoid reprisals from the vindictive Gaullists. An interesting if rather inexplicable fact is that recruitment figures for *Charlemagne* actually quadrupled after it was incorporated into the SS!

The other four national legions were recruited as part of the Waffen-SS

A youthful member of the Legion Norwegen.

Danish volunteers in the SS on the parade ground.

Above *An officer congratulates members of the* Legion Nederland *who have been awarded the Iron Cross.*

Above *An early volunteer in the* Legion Niederlande.

Below *Norwegian volunteers being sworn into the Waffen-SS.*

from the outset but even though they were permitted their own officers their personnel quickly found, like the earlier volunteers for what became the *Wiking* Division, that promises that they would be treated in identical fashion to German SS troops were rather hollow. There were, in fact, so many complaints about mistreatment and abuse that Himmler had to intervene personally before the volunteers' morale crumbled completely.

In Holland and Belgium, where the formation of a new volunteer regiment, Freiwilligen Standarte *Nordwest*, had already started, the men were now divided to form the cadres of two national legions, Freiwilligen Legionen *Flandern* and *Niederland*. Similarly, and despite the objection of the Danish government, the Freiwilligenverband *Danemark* was created in mid-July, and the Freiwilligen Legion *Norwegen* at the end of the month. After training in Poland, *Niederland* and *Flandern* were despatched to the Leningrad front in November, followed by the Danes and Norwegians in spring 1942. The Dutch in particular established a creditable fighting reputation and in common with other developments already noted, in July 1943 were expanded and redesignated the 4th SS-Freiwilligen Panzergrenadier Brigade *Nederland*. After suffering heavy losses during the long retreat from Leningrad back through the Baltic states to Kurland, whence survivors were evacuated by sea, the unit was again renamed as the 23rd SS-Freiwilligen Panzergrenadier Division *Nederland* and was virtually destroyed in the final defence of Berlin.

The Dutch Legion had, for a brief time before being given the status of an independent brigade, been incorporated in the new 11th SS-Freiwilligen Panzergrenadier Division *Nordland* whose creation Hitler had authorized at the end of 1942. Built around the *Nordland* Standarte from the 5th SS-Panzergrenadier Division *Wiking* which formed two battalions of a rechristened Standarte *Norge*, the division incorporated the survivors from the Danish and Norwegian Legions, the former as the new Standarte *Danmark* and the latter as the third battalion in Standarte *Norge*. Additional numbers were made up from Hungarian and Romanian recruits and German officers. The division fought alongside the Dutch Brigade as part of III (*Germanische*) SS Korps during the long retreat to Kurland, whence its survivors were also eventually evacuated by sea, and was finally annihilated by the Red Army in Berlin.

The last of the original legions, *Flandern*, so disgraced itself in combat that in 1943 it was disbanded and those survivors who had not served out their enlistment period were redistributed amongst other SS formations.

* * *

The autumn of 1942 marked the high point of German expansion. In North Africa, Rommel was only a day's drive from the Nile but blocked by the El Alamein Line, while in Russia Stalingrad seemed on the point of falling, German mountain troops had planted the Swastika flag on the summit of Mount Elbrus — highest peak in the Caucasus — and the

Gunners of the Wiking *Division with a 15 cm sIG 33 artillery piece during the summer of 1942.*

Maikop oilfields had been overrun even though Russian technicians had fired the wells. Now the tide turned. Rommel was defeated by Montgomery at the second battle of Alamein at the end of October and forced to retreat at the beginning of November, while on 8 November Anglo-American forces landed behind his back in Morocco and Algeria. Within six months the Axis forces in Africa, driven inexorably back behind a steadily shrinking line in Tunisia, would be forced to surrender and the Allies would have landed on Sicily to begin the reconquest of Europe.

In Stalingrad Sixth Army, despite occupying 90 per cent of the city, would be cut off by Zhukov's new winter counter-offensive which sliced decisively through its flanking Italian and Romanian divisions and, despite relief attempts masterminded by Field Marshal Erich von Manstein in which *Wiking* played a part, would be forced to surrender at the beginning of February 1943. To prevent their own encirclement, the troops in the Caucasus region would also be forced to fall back, some into the Kuban Peninsula (in which the marvellous film *Cross of Iron* is set) whence they would eventually be evacuated across the Kerch Straits into the Crimea, others (including *Wiking*) back through Rostov for the second and last time and then all the way back to Kharkov. Meanwhile, on the other side of the world the Americans won what has come to be seen as the turning point of the Pacific war at the battle of Midway. From this point on, despite inevitable reverses, Allied victory was assured.

Above *Dinner at Bad Tölz during the winter of 1942. Conditions were rather different at Stalingrad...*

Right *A sheepskin jacket and woollen gloves may not have looked smart, but warmth was more important.*

5

Nemesis 1943-5

Even though in retrospect it can clearly be seen that the winter of 1942–3 marked the real beginning of the end for Nazi Germany and its allies, this was far from apparent at the time, especially to the Waffen-SS whose greatest period of expansion was at hand. True, the situation in North Africa (where no SS units were involved) was serious, but Rommel had

Left *Fritz Klingenberg, wearing the Knights Cross awarded for the capture of Belgrade, at the time of the battles around Kharkov.*

Above right *Fritz Witt,* later commander of the 12th SS Panzer Division Hitler Jugend, *was a regimental commander in the Leibstandarte at the time of the battles at Kharkov.*

Right *'Sepp' Dietrich photographed at approximately the same time.*

bounced back before and in any case Hitler mistakenly regarded the campaign there as a 'sideshow', so was not overly concerned. True, too, Sixth Army had been decimated and its survivors herded into captivity at Stalingrad, while the Russian winter offensive had also made significant headway elsewhere, but it *had* been checked and the shortened lines actually gave the Germans a temporary advantage. They were not slow to exploit this, and the Waffen-SS divisions were to have a starring role in the spring and summer operations of 1943.

As at the beginning of the previous year, the Russians had driven the Germans back on a wide front and had actually succeeded in recapturing Kharkov in the middle of February. The Soviet high command, STAVKA, firmly believed they had the Germans on the run at this point. But the three SS divisions Leibstandarte *Adolf Hitler*, *Das Reich* and *Totenkopf* had been returned to the front by this time as the new I SS Panzer Korps, commanded by Paul Hausser, *Das Reich* having passed temporarily to Georg Keppler. *Das Reich* was almost cut off in Kharkov but was withdrawn by Hausser just in time — against Hitler's direct orders. At the same time leading Russian reconnaissance parties reached the eastern bank of the River Dnieper, full of confidence. But the Soviet forces were overstretched, the men tired, the vehicles constantly breaking down and the supply lines inadequate because the Germans had methodically converted the railway lines to European gauge as they advanced and Russian engineers were

Left *Paul Hausser in the turret of a PzKpfw III. (Panzerkampfwagen or armoured fighting vehicle was the standard German name for a tank.)*

Above right Totenkopf *tanks and grenadiers on the outskirts of Kharkov.*

Right *Street fighting in Kharkov. These warm parkas were only issued to Waffen-SS troops; the Army did not have an equivalent.*

Himmler personally flew out to congratulate the men of I SS Panzer Korps after the successful recapture of Kharkov, and he is seen here with officers and men of the 2nd SS Panzer Regiment.

having to convert them back before their own trains could reach the front.

Looking at the strained Russian lines, Field Marshal Erich von Manstein — newly appointed commander of the retitled Army Group Don in southern Russia — decided on a virtual replay of Fedor von Bock's strategy of spring 1942. With First and Fourth Panzer Armies (including *Wiking*) and the help of I SS Panzer Korps, Manstein decided he had sufficient strength to give the Russians a bloody nose before the spring thaw brought a halt to operations. This would then allow him five or six weeks in which to rebuild his strength yet again for a renewed summer offensive. Hitler, shaken by the disaster at Stalingrad and temporarily unsure of his own infallibility, was not convinced, and even flew out to Manstein's head-quarters at Zaporozhye on 17 February to argue against his plans. Manstein proved persuasive, though, and the Führer gave his approval two days later, a decision which may have been hastened by a report of Russian tanks only half a dozen miles away!

The Manstein plan was classically simple. First and Fourth Panzer Armies would assemble between Zaporozhye and Krasnoarmeskoye, south-east of Dnepropetrovsk, while I SS Panzer Korps would be to the north-east around Krasnograd. Fourth Army and the SS Korps would converge in the general direction of Pavlograd to cut off the leading elements of the Soviet Sixth Army while First Panzer Army attacked further east through Marshal

Vatutin's so-called Front Mobile Group towards Izyum. The combined forces would then regroup to strike north-east, recapture Kharkov and head towards Kursk.

The operation succeeded brilliantly to begin with. Commencing on 20 February, the German forces stove in Vatutin's, cutting off part of Sixth Army including an entire armoured corps which was stranded for lack of fuel, and by the end of the month had pushed the Russians back behind the River Donets east of Izyum. They then converged on Kharkov, I SS Panzer Korps spearheading the attack, and entered the city on 11 March. Four days of bitter street fighting ensued before the Russians abandoned Kharkov on 15 March. 'The SS Panzer Korps,' declared a revitalized and ecstatic Führer, 'is worth 20 Italian divisions.' The Russians had lost 72,000 men dead and captured and approximately 1,200 tanks, but Soviet tank production was now up to 600–800 a month so these would soon be replaced...

Unfortunately for him, the third phase of Manstein's plan had to be shelved because the temperature had risen unexpectedly early and, as usual, the ground had turned to thick gluey mud over which mobile operations were quite impossible. This meant that there was still a large bulge or salient in the front line around Kursk and south of Orel, the latter being still in German hands.

For the next three months there was comparative quiet on the Eastern Front as both sides recovered their strength after the winter fighting. The Kursk salient became the focus of attention because both could see the

Infantry march past a knocked-out Elefant tank destroyer. This photo was actually taken in Italy after the vehicles had been modified to incorporate a bow machine-gun.

SS grenadiers confer with the commander of a Tiger tank at the beginning of the battle of Kursk.

opportunities (and the dangers) it represented. To the Germans — although Manstein, Guderian and others had misgivings — it offered a chance to destroy substantial Soviet forces and regain the initiative. By 4 May the broad outline of a plan had been agreed. Manstein's forces would assemble south of the salient and thrust northwards while the Ninth Army from Army Group Centre, commanded by Field Marshal Walter Model, would attack from the north. If the two armies could achieve a successful link-up east of Kursk, they would have the best part of two Soviet Army Fronts in the bag. Unfortunately there were constant delays in launching the offensive, most of them caused by Model who was determined not to move until he received the 90 Ferdinand tank destroyers he had been promised.*

Other delays were caused by problems in tank production. During 1942, at Hitler's express wishes, great emphasis had been placed on the

---

* The firms of Porsche and Henschel had both produced prototypes of a new heavy tank mounting an 8.8 cm gun in 1942. The Henschel design was adjudged superior and went into production as the PzKpfw VI, later given the name Tiger. However, Porsche had been overconfident of winning the contract so had already built 90 chassis and hulls. These subsequently had their engines moved to the front and large, heavily armoured superstructures mounting 8.8 cm guns were fitted to the rear. Officially designated Ferdinands, after Professor Ferdinand Porsche, they were also known as Elefants. In action, though, they proved themselves more of white elephants for, lacking even a single machine-gun for self-protection, they were extremely vulnerable to Russian infantry equipped with magnetic anti-tank mines. After the battle of Kursk the surviving vehicles were retrofitted with a bow machine-gun and shipped to Italy.

Above *Festooned with bandoliers and belt pockets of ammunition, grenadiers prepare themselves for the coming battle.*

Below *Little villages no one had ever heard of became strongpoints for Russian troops whom even the SS had difficulty in dislodging.*

Above Totenkopf *personnel scan the horizon from the scant shelter of a ploughed field.*

Left *An unshaven* Das Reich *grenadier peers through the sunflowers.*

Above right *Soviet aircraft were a perpetual menace because by this time the Red Air Force had largely recovered from its hammering in 1941 and more modern designs dedicated to the ground attack role were in service. Here, SS troops man a pair of machine-guns on an anti-aircraft mounting.*

manufacture of tank destroyers at the expense of the standard PzKpfw III and IV medium tanks. Then came the introduction of the Tiger to confuse the issue further, while work had also started on the even newer PzKpfw V Panther, a heavy medium tank designed to be able to take on the T–34 at equal odds. All this, coupled with increasing Allied bombing of German industry, dissipated the war effort despite the work of Heinz Guderian, who was appointed Inspector-General of Armoured Troops in February 1943, and Armaments Minister Albert Speer. Meanwhile, the Russians simply continued to churn out hundreds of the excellent and proven T–34 each month.

Even while the plans for the new German offensive were being firmed up, Manstein expressed his worries to Hitler. 'How many people,' he asked, 'do you think even know where Kursk is? It's a matter of profound indifference to the world whether we hold Kursk or not.' Manstein was one of the few German Generals who still dared to talk this bluntly to the Führer. 'You're quite right,' the dictator replied. 'Whenever I think of this attack my stomach turns over.' Hitler should have listened to his own gut feeling, for Operation *Zitadelle* ('Citadel'), as it was codenamed, proved a disaster.

Just as the Germans had seen the opportunities presented by the Kursk Salient, so had the Russians. There were two Army Fronts within the 'bulge', Vatutin's and Rokossovksy's. If they were reinforced and well dug in, they could blunt the predictable German offensive and provide a springboard for a Soviet autumn counter-attack. To this end, Marshal Georgi Zhukov conscripted some 300,000 people from towns and villages

Left *To prevent being strafed by the Luftwaffe, SS grenadiers wave frantically and display a Swastika flag.*

Below *The summer heat and endless miles of grainfields soon began to exert their toll on tired and underfed troops.*

Below right *Even when an armoured personnel carrier was available to give their feet a rest, the strain of battle was apparent.*

around Kursk to start digging trenches, tank traps and laying minefields. The salient's perimeter was 345 miles long and because the defence was designed in depth in concentric battle lines two to three miles deep, this meant digging no less than 6,000 miles of trenches! The minefields were cleverly designed to funnel the German tanks into 'killing grounds' where well dug-in and camouflaged anti-tank guns could have a skeet shoot. By the time the German offensive opened on 5 July, the Russians had three Army Fronts in the salient with three Tank Armies as a mobile reserve, a force of roughly 1,300,000 men, 3,600 tanks and tank destroyers, 20,000 artillery pieces and 2,400 aircraft.

Opposing them was Model's Ninth Army in the north with four Panzer divisions plus the 505th schwere Panzer Abteilung (heavy tank battalion) and the 653rd and 654th Ferdinand Battalions; holding a defensive line on the western edge of the salient was Second Army; while in the south Manstein had Fourth Panzer Army, Operational Detachment Kempf and the SS Panzer Korps, including nine Panzer divisions and the 503rd Heavy Tank Battalion. In addition, each of the three SS divisions had an integral company of Tiger tanks (13 to 15 vehicles), as did the Army's *Großdeutschland* Division. This represented a total force of approximately 900,000 men, 2,700 tanks, assault guns and tank destroyers, 10,000 artillery pieces and 2,000 aircraft. Even though attacking an enemy in

Left *NCOs confer over a map. The man kneeling is holding a captured Russian PPSh-41 sub-machine-gun.*

Right *Here come the tanks!*

Below right *PzKpfw IIIs and IVs with infantry in half-tracks press furiously forward.*

prepared positions with inferior forces of your own is obviously undesirable and often fatal, the Germans did have one advantage in the choice of time and place for their attack. However, they could not hope to conceal their preparations completely and as it happened a Hungarian deserter gave the Russians the exact time of Model's H-Hour, allowing them to pre-empt the assault with a massive artillery bombardment on Ninth Army as the troops were moving up to their start lines at 02:20 on 5 July. This caused considerable confusion as well as casualties and a 90 minute delay, which was just a foretaste of worse to come.

In the north, despite all his elaborate preparations, Model was only able to make minimal headway. By the end of the second day of the attack his forces had only advanced nine or ten miles and within a week he had lost half his armour to no effect. The Ferdinands he had delayed the assault for proved next to useless in an offensive role and the new Panthers suffered from a high breakdown rate — the penalty for rushing untried designs into a major battle.

In the south the offensive at first seemed to make better headway. Here, Kempf's battlegroup had achieved surprise south-east of Belgorod by starting its attack during the afternoon of 4 July, an unusual and therefore unexpected time of day to launch a major offensive. His attack cleared a ridge which gave him a springboard for the following day. The tanks

Above *A StuG III passes a wounded soldier.*

Below *Tiger tanks of the* Das Reich *Division displaying the special tactical marking devised for Operation* Zitadelle.

Above *Another Tiger from the same unit passes a couple of exhausted grenadiers.*

Below *The new PzKpfw V Panthers looked sleek and powerful but suffered from many mechanical defects.*

Above *Here, with the tide of battle beginning to turn, a Panther has been hastily camouflaged to await the Russian onslaught.*

Below *The crew of a* Das Reich *PzKpfw III pose beside their tank during the battle.*

Above *Grenadiers take temporary shelter in a captured Russian trench.*

Below *A 7.5 cm PaK 40 anti-tank gun in action.*

clattered forward under cover of darkness but daylight brought unseasonal rain which slowed their advance, and here the Soviet anti-tank guns were particularly well concealed in wooded country which was hardly ideal for mobile operations in any case. As a result, Kempf was unable to break through the first defence line until 8 July.

To his east the three divisions of I SS Panzer Korps had made much more rapid progress, pushing ahead some 15 miles on the first day, breaking through the first defence line as far as Pokrovka. The tanks were deployed in wedge-shaped formations with the heavier Tigers and Panthers in the lead supported by the lighter and less well-armed PzKpfw IIIs and IVs to their rear. Their next objective was Prokhorovka on the Belgorod-Kursk railway line, after which the intention was to force a crossing of the River Psel and attack Kursk from the south-east. After the first day, however, the attack was slowed up, partly because of the need to allow flanking Army units to catch up and partly because of stiffening Soviet opposition.

On Hausser's left, General Hermann Hoth's XLVIII Panzer Korps was heading generally in the direction of Oboyan. Here, Vatutin's defences were particularly strong as he intended to funnel the Panzers into a narrow wedge of ground where they would be unable to manoeuvre properly. Moreover, the rain had swollen a stream across their path into a torrent while the *Großdeutschland* Division's brand-new Panther battalion had the misfortune to run slap into an uncharted minefield. The Korps fought its way to the River Pena on 8 July and some units managed to cross it before being thrown back. Hoth therefore diverted his line of advance north-westward to parallel that of Hausser's, reaching Novoselovka on 10 July. Similarly, on the right flank Kempf found himself channelled north towards Rzhavets.

By the time Kempf reached Rzhavets on 10 July, the *Totenkopf* Division had forced a crossing of the Psel, which was the last natural defensive line in front of Kursk, and the three SS divisions were deployed around Prokhorovka and Krasny Oktyobar. Victory seemed almost within grasp, but psychologically the troops were looking over their shoulders, because news had arrived of the Anglo-American landings on Sicily on 10 July. Picking his moment with care, Vatutin hurled the whole of General Nikolai Rotmistrov's Fifth Guards Tank Army into a counter-attack on 12 July, a force of some 850 T–34s, KV–1s and SU–85 tank destroyers. Throughout the morning the three SS divisions withstood the onslaught on their own while Hoth's XLVIII Panzer Korps struggled to reach them; Kempf was still 12 miles away, though, and unable to add his weight to the battle.

The SS tank crews fought with all their customary skill and determination but they were compressed into an area only some three miles square which denied them the ability to manoeuvre, as Vatutin had planned. Then the Russian tanks charged them at full speed so as to deny the Tigers and Panthers their usual advantage of weapons' range. The T–34s swarmed all around the Panzers, firing into their flanks at distances measured in tens rather than hundreds of yards. Orchards and cornfields were blackened with fire and littered with burnt-out wrecks of tanks. Both sides displayed suicidal courage: tanks which had expended all their ammunition deliberately rammed other vehicles and their crews fought it out with smallarms or hand to hand.

The battle lasted for over eight hours and in the end it was Rotmistrov who called off the attack, having lost more than half his tanks. (Thirty were destroyed by a single Tiger, that commanded by Michael Wittmann of the Leibstandarte who would eventually emerge as the highest scoring tank 'ace' of the war.) But it was a Pyrrhic victory for the Germans, who had lost over 300 of their own armoured fighting vehicles, and Operation *Zitadelle* had to be abandoned, not least because the Russians now launched a new counter-offensive of their own towards Orel which threatened to cut off Model's Ninth Army unless it retreated hastily. Moreover, Hitler was demanding reinforcements for the Italian Front, including the Leibstandarte, so Manstein really had no alternative. From now on, despite local successes, the German Army on the Eastern Front would be in full retreat, a retreat which would end in the blackened rubble of Berlin.

* * *

Men of the Prinz Eugen *Division prepare to scale a rock face.*

Otto Kumm attempted unsuccessfully to whip Prinz Eugen *into a decent fighting formation.*

A smiling Sturmbannführer wearing the Prinz Eugen *cuff title.*

Even while these dramatic events were taking place on the seemingly endless Russian steppes, the Waffen-SS was going through a paroxysm of growth. We have seen in the previous chapter how the various Western European Legions and anti-Communist volunteers from the Baltic States and the Ukraine were incorporated eventually under Himmler's *Sigrunen* banner, but they were not alone.

By March 1942 the nucleus of what was to become the 7th SS-Frei-willigen Gebirgs Division *Prinz Eugen* had been raised from men of Germanic extraction living in the Balkans, some Romanian, some Serbian and Croatian. The original members were volunteers, but from mid-1942 a form of quasi-legal 'volunteer or else' conscription was introduced for the *Volksdeutsche* (ethnic Germans) living in occupied and satellite countries, which caused a predictable decline in discipline and standards. *Prinz Eugen* was predominantly employed throughout the war in 'security' operations against Tito's partisans in Yugoslavia, but was reluctantly engaged against the Russians around Belgrade in October 1944. It was a second-rate formation not to be classed alongside the Leibstandarte, *Das Reich*, *Totenkopf* or *Wiking*, and its personnel largely form the stereotype of the 'SS thug'. They were brutal in search and reprisal operations against civilians but could not stand up to trained troops in a straight battle, and as the war dragged to a close the number of desertions multiplied dramatically.

An SS cavalry detachment on patrol.

Brigadeführer Otto Kumm, one of the Waffen-SS's most popular and tenacious Generals, tried to instil some professional *esprit de corps* into the division when he assumed command in February 1944, but it was a hopeless cause. As the Americans found in Vietnam, reluctant conscripts generally make uncommitted soldiers. The division's survivors surrendered to the Yugoslavs in May 1945 and large numbers were subsequently executed for war crimes in which rape, torture and wanton murder of women and children featured heavily. Many ex-members of the premier SS divisions will talk happily and with pride of their accomplishments; most members of *Prinz Eugen* tend to stay quiet.

Much the same can be said about the 8th SS-Kavallerie Division *Florian Geyer*, raised as we have seen earlier from *Totenkopf* cavalry regiments. Its original commander while it was still just a brigade was Hermann Fegelein, who later married Eva Braun's sister Gretl.* He was succeeded by Wilhelm Bittrich until the latter assumed command of the 9th SS Panzer Division (see below), whereupon Fegelein resumed command until transferred to the Führer Headquarters in 1944. This division also spent most of the war in anti-partisan duties either behind the lines in Russia or in the Balkans. In

---

* The relationship with Hitler's mistress and eventual wife did not save him from execution when he was accused of desertion in April 1945.

Left *SdKfz 222 armoured car of the* Florian Geyer Division.

Left *Hermann Fegelein in September 1943.*

Right *'Willi' Bittrich addressing men of the newly formed 9th SS Panzer Division* Hohenstaufen *in September 1943.*

the summer of 1943 it formed part of Ninth Army and following the failure of the Kursk operation was transferred to the southern sector of the front. After a brief rest during the winter of 1943–44 it ceased to exist as a division except on paper, its component elements being dispersed throughout the Balkans, Hungary and Poland. The division's remnants were annihilated in Budapest in 1945.

Keeping in numerical sequence, of considerably more significance in military terms than either of the above formations were the 9th and 10th SS Divisions *Hohenstaufen* and *Frundsberg*. Raised in late 1942/early 1943 from eighteen-year-old conscripts with a cadre of veterans from the Leibstandarte and *Das Reich*, they spent a year training up and emerged in spring 1944 as fully fledged Panzer divisions, seeing action on both the Eastern and Western Fronts during 1944–45 as described later. Their commanders were Gruppenführer Wilhelm Bittrich and Brigadeführer Karl von Treuenfeld. These were both purely German formations, not foreign volunteer organizations, and their fighting record pays tribute to the calibre of German youth even at this late stage in the war. The 12th SS Panzer Division *Hitler Jugend* falls in the same category. The brainchild of the Hitler Youth leader, Artur Axmann, it was given Hitler's blessing in February 1943 and activated in June. Its recruits were seventeen-year-old volunteers from the Hitler Youth formed around a cadre of experienced officers and NCOs from other divisions and commanded by Standartenführer (later Brigadeführer) Fritz Witt, a dashing and daring

officer. The division later distinguished itself in Normandy and the Ardennes.

The word 'distinguished' cannot be applied to the 13th Waffen Gebirgs Division der SS *Handschar* (kroatische Nr 1) which was raised in the spring of 1943 around a cadre from *Prinz Eugen* and was composed of Moslems from the Bosnian populace of Yugoslavia who were traditional enemies of the Christian Serbs who themselves formed the bulk of the partisan forces. The Croats were permitted to continue to observe their religious and dietary obligations, a strange quirk on Himmler's part but by this stage of the war he needed manpower more than anything else. Wearing their usual fezes, but in field grey in common with the rest of their uniform instead of the traditional red, these 'Croatian' SS volunteers (many of whom were actually conscripted under threat of punishment) rivalled *Prinz Eugen* in terms of atrocities and desertions. The latter reached epidemic proportions with the advance of the Red Army in 1944 and the division was disbanded in October/November of that year, although the honour title was kept in existence for a regimental-size battlegroup of ethnic Germans (the 13th SS-Gebirgs Regiment Gruppe *Handschar*) which fought on to the war's end. The title was also used as a cover name to deceive the Russians when the elite 16th SS Panzergrenadier Division *Reichsführer-SS* (see below) was transferred from Italy to Hungary during the desperate closing days of the war.

Left *Fritz Witt* (centre) *with Joachim Peiper — the man later convicted for the Malmédy massacre — on his right, seen in Kharkov in March 1943.*

Above right *The Grand Mufti of Jerusalem with Aserbaidschan (Azer- baijani) Moslem volunteers in the SS.*

The *Handschar* Division is a good example of how the Waffen-SS had deteriorated from its early high ideals by 1943. Unfortunately it is not alone. Attempts were made in 1944 to form two further Moslem divisions, the 21st Waffen Gebirgs Division der SS *Skanderberg* (albanische Nr 1) and the 23rd *Kama* (kroatische Nr 2). The Albanian 'division' never exceeded 6,500 men and mass desertions reduced this after a month of combat to 1,300 so Himmler disbanded it in disgust in October 1944, transferring its few reliable personnel to *Prinz Eugen*. *Kama* never existed as a division except on paper since the rapid Russian advance during the autumn of 1944 made recruitment impossible. The few recruits who had been assembled were transferred to the 13th SS-Gebirgs Regiment Gruppe *Handschar*.

The other foreign SS divisions were the 18th SS-Freiwilligen Panzergrenadier Division *Horst Wessel* (named after the SA stormtrooper who wrote the Nazi marching song which became known as the 'Horst Wessel Song' after he was killed in a brawl with Communists in 1930); the 22nd SS-Freiwilligen Kavallerie Division *Maria Theresia*; the 24th Waffen Gebirgs Division der SS *Karstjäger*; the 25th and 26th Waffen Grenadier Divisionen *Hunyadi* (ungarische Nr 1) and *Hungaria* or *Gömbös* (Nr 2); the 27th SS-Freiwilligen Grenadier Division *Langemarck* (flämische Nr 1); the 29th Waffen Grenadier Division der SS (italienische Nr 1); the 31st SS-Freiwilligen Grenadier Division *Böhmen-Mähren*; the 33rd Waffen Kavallerie Division der SS (ungarische Nr 3); and the 34th SS-Grenadier Division *Landstorm Nederland*. These were of very mixed size and calibre.

The 18th, 22nd, 25th, 26th, 31st and 33rd Divisions were principally created from Hungarian *Volksdeutsche* volunteers and, later, conscripts, but only the 18th was ever fully formed. Raised in spring 1944, it undertook some anti-partisan duties but spent most of the remainder of the war fighting the Red Army on the central front, retreating from Budapest finally to surrender near Prague at the end of the war. The 22nd Division only consisted of two regiments, one seconded from *Florian Geyer* and the other from a Hungarian cavalry regiment. The honour title is unconfirmed. It was destroyed alongside *Florian Geyer* in Budapest. The 25th was in the process of being formed in the summer of 1944 but it was decimated during the Soviet autumn offensive. The 26th and 31st Divisions were formed from German and Hungarian stragglers during the winter of 1944 but were never divisions except in name (the *Hungaria* and/or *Gömbös* honour titles are also unconfirmed), while the 33rd (confusingly bearing the same number as the French SS *Charlemagne* Division) was just a single regiment raised for the defence of Budapest and was destroyed there.

The 24th and 29th Divisions were both formed in Italy. When the Italians formally signed the armistice on 29 September 1943 an isolated SS security battalion found itself the nucleus of a brigade-sized 'division' into which *Volksdeutsche* from the Southern Tyrol were recruited. Although engaged principally in anti-partisan duties, the *Karstjäger* Division saw some action against British troops in the Julian Alps before surrendering in May 1945. The 29th Division took over the number of the disgraced and disbanded 'Kaminski Brigade' in September 1944. Its personnel were Italian fascists from the *Milizia Armata*, but little is known of its composition or activities except that the latter were mostly anti-partisan.

In May 1943 a new Flemish unit was raised to replace the similarly disgraced and disbanded Flemish Legion and given the title 6th SS-Freiwilligen Sturmbrigade *Langemarck*. Unlike its predecessor, it fought well and suffered heavy losses around Zhitomir in spring 1944, after which it was withdrawn to Czechoslovakia for rest and refit. Replacement personnel were drawn from a wide variety of non-SS sources, including Luftwaffe, Kriegsmarine and Organization Todt people! Although given divisional status in September 1944, it was really little more than a reinforced regiment whose remnants surrendered at Mecklenburg in 1945. Similarly, in September 1944 the Dutch security regiment *Landwacht Niederlande* was incorporated into the Waffen-SS and graced with a divisional number and title. It fought alongside *Hohenstauffen* and *Frundsberg* at Arnhem but was otherwise chiefly engaged in operations against the Dutch Resistance until the end of the war.

Of much greater significance than these ad hoc late war 'volunteer' formations were the 16th and 17th SS-Panzergrenadier Divisionen *Reichsführer-SS* and *Götz von Berlichingen*. Composed principally of Germans and Austrians with some Balkan *Volksdeutsche*, they both established fine fighting reputations. *Reichsführer-SS* (Himmler's pet formation) was based upon the Sturmbrigade *Reichsführer-SS* which was on Corsica at the time of the Allied invasion of Sicily. It was brought back to the mainland to be expanded to the size of a division in October, commanded first by

StuG III assault guns of the 16th SS-Panzergrenadier Division Reichsführer-SS *in Italy.*

Brigadeführer Max Simon, Theodor Eicke's former deputy in *Totenkopf*, and later by Oberführer Otto Baum, one of the most highly decorated officers in Germany and the holder of the Knights Cross with Oakleaves, Swords and Diamonds. Part of the division fought at Anzio in February 1944, while the remainder helped in the occupation of Hungary in March after Hitler came to suspect that the Regent, Admiral Miklós Horthy, was secretly seeking a separate peace with Stalin — which, indeed, he was.

To digress briefly, although it is still very much part of the story of the Waffen-SS, a second reason for the occupation, totally non-military, was the status of Hungarian Jews. Because Hungary was an ally of however dubious status rather than an occupied country, its people had enjoyed a fragile self-government ever since joining the Axis. Under this, while Jews were officially regarded as second-class citizens, they were neither herded into concentration camps nor ghettos but allowed to survive as best they could without too much overt harassment, a state of affairs which Hitler, Himmler and Eichmann found intolerable. Now the Hungarian Jews would feel the power of the *Einsatzgruppen* and be herded to their extermination in their hundreds of thousands while a thoroughly intimidated Horthy washed his hands of the affair. Later, following the collapse of Romania and Bulgaria in August, Horthy continued his covert negotiations and on 15 October made a radio broadcast openly asking for an armistice with Russia. The SS commando Otto Skorzeny* kidnapped his son Nikolaus and after a brief show of resistance Horthy meekly abdicated and allowed himself to be flown to Berlin where he was placed under house arrest, while his country was forced to endure a puppet government until overrun by the Russians. (Horthy was interned after the war and subsequently lived in exile in Portugal, where he died in 1957.)

The 16th SS-Panzergrenadier Division *Reichsführer-SS* was reunited in Italy in May-June 1944 to help resist the inexorable Allied advance after the eventual capture of Monte Cassino and the fall of Rome. Part of the division was responsible for one of the worst atrocities of the war when, in reprisal for partisan attacks, 2,700 villagers from Monte Sole were wantonly slain. (Max Simon was sentenced to death at Nürnberg but the sentence was commuted to life imprisonment and in fact he was released in 1954.) In December the division was transferred to Hungary where it was decimated in the battle of Lake Balaton during the attempt to relieve Budapest; the survivors fled westwards and surrendered to British and American troops near Klagenfurt.

The 17th SS-Panzergrenadier Division *Götz von Berlichingen* (named after a medieval robber baron!) worked up in France during late 1943/early 1944 and was rushed to Normandy after D-Day, first seeing action on 11 June at Carentan against the US 82nd and 101st Airborne Divisions. It tried to stem the American breakout at Avranches and was practically annihilated in the Falaise pocket, survivors being amalgamated into the 2nd SS-Panzer Division *Das Reich*. It was rebuilt around two Panzergrenadier Brigades originally earmarked for the 26th and 27th SS Divisions and was thrown into the battle of Metz in November, losing three-quarters of its 16,000 men. The remnants fought in the Saar battles until March 1945, survivors retreating to Nürnberg and finally surrendering near Achensee in May.

The remaining SS divisions were very much 'divisions' in name only. The 32nd SS-Freiwilligen Grenadier Division *30 Januar* was created in January

* Otto Skorzeny was a larger than life character whose exploits have become legendary and to a degree typify the devil-may-care attitude of the Waffen-SS, even though in his post-war writings Skorzeny claimed undue credit for achievements which were not solely his. Born in 1908, he originally wanted to join the Luftwaffe but opted for the SS instead because his 6 ft 6 in frame made him ineligible for aircrew. Apart from the kidnapping of Horthy's son, he is mainly remembered for the rescue of Mussolini from the hotel where he was being kept prisoner at Gran Sasso following the Italian collapse in 1943 (whereas real credit belongs to Luftwaffe paratroops); for the daring though unsuccessful raid on Tito's headquarters in 1944; for helping to stop the July 1944 bomb plot by his prompt action against the conspirators; and for leading the 150th Brigade in captured American uniforms and vehicles during the 'Battle of the Bulge' in December 1944. He defended himself skilfully at Nürnberg and was acquitted, after which he claimed responsibility for organizing the 'Odessa' escape line for Nazis on the run popularized by novelist Frederick Forsyth. Skorzeny died in 1975, still much of an enigma.

Otto Skorzeny.

Werner Ostendorff, the first commander of Götz von Berlichingen, *actually photographed earlier in 1941.*

1945 from stragglers and staff from training schools and was approximately the size of a regiment. It was destroyed during the final defence of Berlin. The 35th SS-Polizei Grenadier Division, another regiment-sized unit, was formed in February 1945 from the Dresden police force and staff from Braunschweig. It fought with Fourth Panzer Army in the closing weeks of the war and surrendered to the Russians at Halbe. The 37th SS-Freiwilligen Kavallerie Division *Lützow* was formed in February/March 1945 from survivors of the 8th and 22nd SS-Kavallerie Divisions plus other stragglers and fought north of Vienna at the war's end, surrendering to the Americans in May. The 38th SS-Grenadier Division *Nibelungen* was formed in March 1945 from staff from Bad Tölz, German survivors from the 30th SS Division when the Russian personnel were attached to Vlasov's Army, and a number of under-age volunteers. It saw limited action in Bavaria before the war's end.

To round off this section, three other Waffen-SS formations must briefly be mentioned. First is the so-called 36th Waffen Grenadier Division der SS. It was formed with Gottlob Berger's help by a convicted sex offender and alcoholic, Standartenführer Dr Oskar Dirlewanger, in 1940 for anti-partisan duties in Poland. Its original personnel were all convicts as well and its ranks were later swelled by men released on parole from military and civilian prisons and concentration camps. With this background, it will come as no surprise to learn that the 'Dirlewanger Brigade', as it was more commonly known, had an atrocity record only rivalled by Kaminski's men alongside whom it fought in suppressing the Warsaw Uprising in 1944. Incredibly, Dirlewanger was awarded the Knights Cross for his part in this operation! Wounded in February 1945, Dirlewanger was murdered by an unknown person or persons while in an Allied prison hospital in June. His 'brigade' was massacred by the Red Army.

The second of these formations was only nominally a part of the Waffen-SS and does not appear ever to have been given a divisional number or name. In 1941 the militant anti-British Indian terrorist Subhas Chandra Bose sought German help in securing Indian independence. Seeing propaganda value in Bose, the OKW authorized the creation of an Indian Legion formed principally from prisoners-of-war captured in North Africa and, later, Italy. The 'Legion', which eventually grew to a strength of some 2,000 men, never actually saw battle. It did occupation duty in France until the Allied invasion, retreated hastily to Germany and was formally inducted into the SS but remained safely out of the fighting!

The last unit to record is the *Britische Freikorps*. In 1943, following his success in recruiting volunteers of other nationalities from prisoner-of-war camps, Gottlob Berger decided to try to raise a British Legion to fight in Russia. His principal ally was John Amery, a member of Oswald Mosley's fascist Blackshirt movement and son of a distinguished British Peer. Amery had earlier tried to interest the Wehrmacht in his ideas but without success. Now, though, Berger agreed that Amery could go around PoW camps seeking volunteers and had some recruiting leaflets printed. Exaggerated

Members of the 'Dirlewanger Brigade' in Warsaw.

stories about the size of the *Freikorps* stem from the fact that the SS established a recreation centre outside Berlin to which prisoners who expressed any interest were sent for a 'holiday' where the better food and living conditions might encourage them. Unknown to the Germans, British camp officers deliberately sent many men off for these holidays, particularly the sick who would benefit from a spell in better circumstances. They were also instructed to observe and report back on the conditions they observed generally during their train journeys, and on the state of German morale, etc. Apparently, some 300 men took advantage of the SS's offer, but it is gratifying to note that only 58 men actually joined the *Freikorps*.

They were kitted out in field grey with SS-style collar patches bearing three silver leopards as their insignia and a Union Jack armshield. Basically a propaganda unit, the *Freikorps* was never used seriously in combat although some 20 volunteers were briefly attached to the 11th SS-Freiwilligen Panzergrenadier Division *Nordland* in March 1945 when one man was wounded. He was awarded a Wound Badge, the only Briton to be given a Nazi military decoration (although many influential Britons who supported Hitler prewar had received political awards). The bulk of the *Freikorps* was captured by the Russians in Stettin and repatriated; Amery himself had fled to Italy with his girlfriend and was captured while in hiding in Milan. Tried by Courts Martial in camera after the war (the transcriptions are still locked away from public examination), most of the

John Amery with his girlfriend at the time of his capture.

Freikorps men pleaded not guilty of treason because they had volunteered to fight Russians, not fellow Britons, and received lenient prison sentences. Amery and a couple of other ringleaders, however, were executed. As a remarkable footnote, shortly after a television interview about one of my earlier books in which a photo of a *Freikorps* man was shown, I received an invitation to visit him where he is living in retirement near Norwich!

* * *

Returning to the Russian Front in the summer of 1943, it remains to be seen how the premier Waffen-SS divisions fared for the remainder of the war, and how their own nemesis overtook them. The Leibstandarte *Adolf Hitler* was unnecessarily hived off to Italy after the battle of Kursk, where its personnel, instead of being thrown into the front line against the Anglo-American invasion forces, were committed to the degrading role of anti-partisan warfare in the north of the country. Atrocity followed; in September the villagers of Boves were wiped out apart from a pitiful handful of accidental survivors. It was later established that Joachim Peiper was the officer responsible, but only after he had been released from prison following his conviction at Nürnberg for the Malmédy massacre during the Battle of the Bulge (see below). 'Sepp' Dietrich, the divisional commander, was disgusted during the Leibstandarte's brief sojourn in Italy with being entrusted to acting as personal escort to Mussolini's mistress, Clara

Pettachi! Fortunately for his own peace of mind, this situation did not last long and the Leibstandarte was soon back in its natural fighting element on the Eastern Front where every reliable fighting man was needed.

Now was the time when the SS divisions would really show their tenacity, skill and fighting spirit, for nothing is more demoralizing or demanding of vigilance and professionalism than a long retreat against seemingly hopeless odds. It took the German Army scant weeks to reach the Ukraine in 1941; it would take the Russian Army nearly two desperate years to push them all the way back.

North of the Kursk salient, the Russian offensive towards Orel hurled Ninth Army and Second Panzer Army back 95 miles to a line just east of Bryansk before the situation was temporarily stabilized. Then, unexpectedly, the Red Army launched a second assault from the direction of Belogorod aiming to drive a wedge between Manstein's weakened Fourth Panzer Army and Operational Detachment Kempf in the south and recapture Kharkov once more. The attack began on 3 August and Manstein only averted complete disaster by throwing his three SS Panzergrenadier divisions *Das Reich*, *Totenkopf* and *Wiking* into the breach. Nevertheless, Kharkov had finally to be abandoned on 22 August, by which time the Red Army had recovered all the ground lost to the Wehrmacht in the spring. Even this was only a prelude to the great Soviet autumn and winter offensives, though.

As soon as it had become obvious that Operation *Zitadelle* was a failure,

Officers and men of the 5th SS Panzer Regiment, Wiking *Division, in the autumn of 1943.*

A knocked-out Wiking *Division SdKfz 251 half-track.*

Hitler had ordered the construction of a fortified defence line grandly named the 'Eastern Rampart' running northwards from the coast of the Sea of Azov south of Melitopol, broadly following the line of the wide and deep River Dnieper through Dnepropetrovsk, Kiev and Gomel, then bending east to encompass Bryansk and Smolensk in Army Group Centre's sector. The Führer was determined to hang on to the western Ukraine and the Crimea, the latter having been designated a resettlement area for racial Germans once victory had been achieved. For the Russians the recapture of Kiev and Smolensk were important for propaganda reasons, but breaking the Eastern Rampart was the strategically more significant objective.

In the southern sector Manstein's Army Group South consisted of First, Fourth and Eighth Panzer Armies plus Sixth and Seventeenth Armies, a total of 68 divisions of which 16 were Panzer or Panzergrenadier. This force of 1,240,000 men and 2,100 tanks and self-propelled guns was opposed by 2,633,000 Russians with 2,400 tanks and assault guns in six Army Fronts: from north to south Marshal Rokossovsky's Central Front, Vatutin's Voronezh Front, Koniev's Steppe Front, Malinkovsky's South-West Front, Tolbukhin's South Front and, in the Taman Peninsula facing across the Kerch Strait into the Crimea, the North Caucasus Front. The Soviet forces began their attack on 26 August and swept rapidly westwards, the SS and Army Panzer divisions fighting stiff rearguard actions to give the slower moving infantry time to retreat behind the Rampart. By 22 September the Russians had reached the Dnieper at several points and began to cross under heavy fire. The important town of Kremenchug, defended by *Das Reich* and the Army's elite *Großdeutschland* Division, was assaulted by three Soviet Armies and carried by storm on 29 September. By the middle of October Dnepropetrovsk had been recaptured while South Front had taken Melitopol and was advancing towards Kherson, sealing off the neck of the Crimea; and by the end of the month the Russians had driven the Germans back from the whole line of the Dnieper apart from a solitary bridgehead around Cherkassy. Kiev, capital of the Ukraine, was finally recaptured on 6 November. Here, though, the assault slowed to a virtual standstill and in the middle of November the Germans were even able to mount a limited counter-attack spearheaded by I SS Panzer Korps* which recaptured Zhitomir.

Meanwhile, on Army Group Centre's front, Marshal Yeremenko's Kalinin Front, Sokolovsky's West Front and Popov's Bryansk Front had launched a simultaneous offensive to recapture Smolensk, Roslavl and Bryansk respectively. Field Marshal von Kluge's forces were seriously outnumbered — some 1,253,000 Russians with 1,400 tanks being opposed by 850,000 Germans with a mere 500 tanks and assault guns — but had the advantage of terrain. The numerous north-south rivers were swollen by the autumn rains and there were many marshy patches and dense woods impassable to armoured fighting vehicles.

The second stage of the Orel offensive opened on 28 August, Yelnya being recaptured after two days. Although the Germans were forced to fall back, they put up a dogged resistance using every natural defensive feature and by the end of the first week in September the Soviet forces had to pause to regroup. They renewed the assault on 14 September, rapidly liberating Bryansk, and a week later had practically encircled Smolensk, forcing Kluge to pull back. Smolensk finally fell on the 25th, the same day that Roslavl was also recaptured after a desperate street by street struggle. When the offensive was brought to a halt on 2 October, the Germans had been driven back between 120 and 150 miles into Belorussia. Now there was a further lull all along the line while the Red Army prepared itself for its third great winter campaign. Anticipating this, Manstein argued persuasively for a withdrawal from the Dnieper bend to shorten the line and free sufficient

* Hausser's original SS Panzer Korps, comprising *Das Reich* and *Totenkopf* in the Leibstandarte's absence in Italy, had been redesignated II SS Panzer Korps. I Korps was formed around the greatly expanded Leibstandarte *Adolf Hitler* while III (Germanische) Panzer Korps under Felix Steiner included *Wiking* and *Nordland*. As new Korps were created to accommodate those SS divisions mentioned earlier which were in the process of being raised, though, divisions were frequently swapped from Korps to Korps according to tactical needs. By the end of 1943 there were six SS Korps — the three already mentioned plus IV SS Panzer Korps under Herbert Gille, V SS Gebirgs Korps which was based in Yugoslavia and VI SS Freiwilligen Korps (the Latvian and Estonian divisions) on the Leningrad front. During 1944 Himmler, appointed commander of the so-called Replacement Army, created seven more SS Korps although, like the late war divisions, most were Korps in name only.

divisions to form a mobile reserve, but Hitler would hear none of it.

The principal objectives of the renewed Soviet attack were to complete the liberation of the Ukraine and Crimea in the south, carrying the war off Russian soil into Romania and Poland, and to drive the Germans back from Leningrad in the north. The operation began on 24 December when Vatutin's renamed 1st Ukrainian Front smashed westwards from its assembly area north of Kiev, rapidly recapturing Zhitomir and within a week driving a 60 mile wedge between First and Fourth Panzer Armies. Manstein riposted with all his usual vigour and succeeded in containing the assault, but his forces had in places been driven back up to 120 miles. Now the Russians started the second stage of the operation, Koniev's 2nd Ukrainian Front striking westward south of the Cherkassy salient. The attack began on 5 January 1944 and made good headway initially, Kirovgrad falling three days later, but then the unexpected strength of the German resistance — and in particular a spirited counter-attack by *Totenkopf* on 16 January — caused Koniev to pause and rethink. The German forces in the salient — the best part of 11 divisions, including *Wiking*, now commanded by Herbert Gille, and Léon Degrelle's Wallonien Brigade, all under the overall command of General Wilhelm Stemmermann — posed a threat to his own northern flank and to Vatutin's southern, so had to be taken out.

Koniev returned to the attack on 25 January, striking north-westward from Kirovgrad and south-westward from Belaya Tserkov, and within four days had completely encircled the German divisions in the salient. Then came an unprecedented change in the weather. The temperature soared, becoming almost spring-like, but making mobile operations totally impossible. Inside the pocket, the German trenches and bunkers were flooded and the airfield at Korsun, into which the Luftwaffe had been ferrying supplies, became so waterlogged it was unusable. Even under these conditions, spirits remained amazingly high and there was even time for humour. Two of Degrelle's men who had been captured were treated to a champagne dinner by a Soviet General and then escorted back through the lines to tell their *Waffenbrüder* that they would receive the same treatment if they surrendered. Needless to say, no one fell for the ruse!

The spirit of optimism declined winter returned and as Koniev steadily tightened the noose around the 50–60,000 Germans, Belgians, Dutchmen, Danes and Norwegians trapped in the pocket. As Degrelle puts it in his memoirs, the 'pocket had the shape of Africa at the end of January. On 9 February, "Africa" had shrunk to "Guinea", actually an area a mere eight by five miles in extent. On this day too, Koniev sent an emissary to Stemmermann calling upon him to surrender, an offer which was curtly refused. Hitler had prohibited a breakout attempt, relying on Manstein to relieve them, but the Field Marshal was faced with an impossible task. The only relatively intact information at his disposal and in a position to help was Hermann Breith's III Panzer Korps comprising the Leibstandarte, 16th and 17th Panzer Divisions and the Heavy Panzer Regiment Bäke

Grenadiers and PzKpfw IVs of the Wiking *Division in the Cherkassy pocket.*

(named after its commander, Lieutenant-Colonel Dr Franz Bäke) with one battalion of Tigers and one of Panthers. However, by this time Koniev had the pocket ringed with some 26 rifle and eight or nine armoured divisions, and Breith was unable to get any closer than eight miles from the south-west corner of the pocket.

Hitler finally agreed to allow the Stemmermann Group to break out and the night of 16/17 February was scheduled for the attempt. *Wiking*, the only Panzer division in the pocket, protected the left flank while Degrelle's Brigade formed the rearguard: only 632 of his 2,000 Walloon volunteers would survive. All the artillery had to be abandoned after the guns had fired off their last remaining ammunition, because it was impossible to tow them through the clinging mud and slush. Even worse, most of the wounded had to be left behind as well, tended by volunteers from the medical staff.

The weary men gathered themselves for this final effort as dusk fell on 16 February and began to move out at 23:00. To begin with things seemed to be going well as the long columns of men and trucks threaded their way through the woods. Leading elements first reached III Panzer Korps' lines at 01:25 on the 17th, but detection was inevitable. Shortly before dawn the Soviet artillery and machine-guns opened fire, the barrage from the dreaded rocket firing *Katyushas* being particularly murderous and turning night into day. A steep-banked river over which there was just a single wooden bridge proved a bottleneck through which the troops stampeded, trampling the dead and wounded underfoot in their desperation to escape. Many men

Léon Degrelle with some of the pitiful survivors of the Wallonien Brigade after the breakout from Cherkassy.

Parade of the Wallonien Brigade in Brussels in April 1944.

shed their uniforms, the better to swim. Tanks stuck in the icy water, unable to move forwards or back. The *Wiking* Division's last 20 tanks turned back to give Degrelle's men a chance to get out of the trap, their crews knowing full well that none of them stood a chance of surviving. The last stragglers, hotly pursued by Cossacks whose sabres took a terrible toll, reached III Panzer Korps at about 16:00. Altogether some 32,000 men managed to escape; a second Stalingrad had been averted even though most of the heavy equipment had been forfeited. General Stemmermann himself was killed in the final fighting. Degrelle, and the *Wiking* division's CO, Herbert Gille, were flown back to Prussia to receive the personal congratulations of Himmler and Hitler; Degrelle was awarded the Knights Cross and Gille the Oakleaves and Swords. Their men were entrained to Poland and given a well-earned 21 days' leaving before remustering to be brought back up to strength and returned to the fray.

*   *   *

The Soviet encirclement of the best part of two German Korps in the Cherkassy salient was an indication of how much the Red Army had learned since 1941, but also of how much it still had to learn. In the summer battles following the German invasion of Russia, literally hundreds of thousands of men had been rounded up by numerically inferior but more skilled soldiers, only comparative handfuls escaping. Now, the Russians were succeeding at last in implementing similar tactics, but having to use vastly superior forces to encircle weaker ones, and even then letting most of them escape (except at Stalingrad, of course). The Soviet command structure was clumsy and even more hampered by political considerations and rivalries than was the German, and the most fanatical bravery on the part of the front line troops could not compensate for lack of proper training and leadership. As 1944 progressed, however, the tables began to turn since millions of Russian soldiers were learning through bitter experience the lessons the German veterans already knew, while the raw youngsters and elderly reservists of Himmler's 'Replacement Army' were largely incapable of responding to the demands imposed on them.

Under these circumstances, Hitler came to rely more and more upon his elite Waffen-SS divisions to stem the tide, but even so it was shortly to be the Leibstandarte's turn to be nearly caught in a trap.

As February turned into March, the Russians continued to press forward on all parts of the front and in the north of Army Group South's sector had actually crossed the pre-1939 Polish frontier, pushing Fourth Panzer Army back to the vicinity of Lvov. General Hans Valentin Hube's First Panzer Army (including the Leibstandarte and a 2,500-man battlegroup from *Das Reich** commanded by Heinz Lammerding) was still holding a line south of Tarnopol against Koniev's 2nd Ukrainian Front, but tanks of Vatutin's 1st Ukrainian Front now swept around its northern flank, cutting off the German lines of communication to the west. If Koniev succeeded in crossing the River Dniester to First Panzer Army's south, Hube's forces would be completely encircled and, indeed, the whole of Army Group South and Field Marshal Ewald von Kleist's Army Group A on its southern flank endangered. Hube was fully aware of the danger and had sent all his wounded and non-combatants westward before the trap was sprung, which it was on 25 March. Manstein had been pleading for First Panzer Army to be allowed to withdraw but up to this point Hitler had refused. Now he relented, leaving First Panzer Army with two choices. Hube wanted to retire to the south-west across the Dniester into Romania, a route taking him through weaker Russian forces than those directly to his west. However, this would have separated First Panzer Army from the rest of Manstein's forces and the Field Marshal therefore insisted on a breakout directly to the west. To help in this, he persuaded Hitler to release Hausser's II SS Panzer Korps which now consisted of the 9th and 10th SS Panzer Divisions *Hohenstaufen* and *Frundsberg*. These had been stationed in France awaiting the Allied invasion which everyone understood was now just a matter of time.

For Manstein, it was both a victory and a defeat since, although the Führer had agreed to his demands, he had had enough of his intractable Field Marshals and on 30 March dismissed him, together with von Kleist, after presenting them both with the Swords to the Knights Cross. (Kleist

---

* The rest of the division had been sent to France for rest and refit in February.

Leibstandarte PzKpfw IVs in the Kamenets-Podolsk pocket.

had conducted a similarly skilful retreat in the face of Hitler's suicidal 'stand at all costs' demands.) At one fell swoop the Führer had deprived the Wehrmacht of two of its most capable senior commanders.* They were replaced by Walter Model and Ferdinand Schörner respectively, neither of whom was of equal calibre although, to give him his due, Model was to show more spirit in the forthcoming defensive battles than he had done at Kursk when entrusted with a primarily offensive operation.

While II SS Korps was entraining for Poland to join Fourth Panzer Army at Tarnopol, the embattled troops in the Kamenets-Podolsk pocket — as it was known, after the most significant town within its perimeter — were kept supplied by the Luftwaffe, fuel being the greatest priority for the tanks, assault guns and artillery tractors. Manstein wanted to prevent the heavy losses in *matériel* which had been caused at Cherkassy by delays in effecting the breakout, and ordered Hube to start his attempt during the night of 27/28 March. Despite a blizzard, the withdrawal made good headway to begin with, the Russians being confused as to its direction, but as they drew in more tanks from north and south the fighting became

* Erich von Manstein was captured by the British at the end of the war, convicted of neglect of civilian life and sentenced to 18 years in prison. He was released on parole in 1952 and settled down to write his memoirs, *Lost Victories* (see *Further reading*). He died peacefully in 1973. Ewald von Kleist was less fortunate. Taken prisoner by the Americans, he was eventually handed over to the Yugoslavs for alleged war crimes. After two years' imprisonment he was passed on to the Russians and died in Soviet captivity in 1954.

tougher. However, Fourth Panzer Army began moving east and leading elements of the two forces met up on 7 April. By 16 April the last stragglers had reached the German lines.

The breakout from the Kamenets-Podolsk pocket was far less traumatic than that from Cherkassy had been and was achieved with considerable skill, Hube's divisions knocking out nearly 400 Soviet tanks and assault guns during the retreat, the Leibstandarte's Tigers and Panthers contributing greatly towards the total. Hube himself was awarded the Diamonds to his Knights Cross with Oakleaves and Swords, but was killed in an air crash on 21 April while flying to receive them.

The Leibstandarte was now sent to Belgium to rest and refit yet again, while survivors from the *Das Reich* battlegroup went to join the rest of their division in France. *Hohenstaufen* and *Frundsberg* were involved in the desperate defence of Tarnopol, which finally fell on 17 April. By this time the spring thaw had brought a halt to mobile operations and the Soviet advance also came to a temporary halt. The two divisions remained in the east until the Allied invasion of Normandy on 6 June, then were transferred to France. But what of the third of the original SS divisions, *Totenkopf*, since the battle of Kursk?

After being thrown out of Kharkov in August 1943 the division — commanded by Max Simon since Eicke's death in February — became part of Eighth Army alongside *Das Reich*. Withdrawn behind the Dnieper in September, the two divisions played a major role in the defence of Kremenchug, then *Totenkopf* was transferred to Schörner's XL Panzer Korps alongside the 14th and 24th Panzer Divisions. (The way in which the Waffen-SS divisions were transferred from Korps to Korps shows how they earned themselves the nickname of the 'Führer's Fire Brigade' on the Russian Front.) Their objective now was the defence of Krivoi Rog, a major rail junction and the communications and supply centre for the southern half of Army Group South which would shortly be taken from Manstein and entrusted to von Kleist as Army Group A.

Totenkopf spearheaded Schörner's counter-attack against Koniev's 2nd Ukrainian Front on 27 October which delayed the capture of the town and Soviet re-occupation of the Dnieper bend by some four months. This is not to say that the struggle died down, for there were furious battles during October and November before *Totenkopf* was transferred again, this time to LVII Korps for yet another successful counter-attack. The pattern of warfare on the Eastern Front was now set: where the Russians rolled the defenders up by sheer weight of numbers, the Germans would create through sheer skill a breathing space like a temporary 'check!' in the game of chess. That was really all they could hope to achieve though, for by this stage of the war the Soviet 'steamroller' was ultimately unstoppable and the eastern European nations which had been annexed by, or allied themselves with, Hitler (however reluctantly) would soon find themselves ruled by a regime equally rigid and inhumane from which they have only just managed to gain a measure of freedom.

In January, as mentioned earlier, *Totenkopf* was in the attacking role again at Kirovgrad and covered Eighth Army's withdrawal, steadily retreating throughout February 1944. (By this time Max Simon had assumed command of the 16th SS Panzergrenadier Division *Reichsführer-SS* in Italy and had been replaced since October 1943 by Hermann Priess.) In March the division was withdrawn behind the Dniester and fought a constant rearguard action all the way back to the Carpathian Mountains in Romania during April. With the coming of the spring lull, the weary troops were able to enjoy something of a rest for a couple of months while Himmler scraped up reinforcements, but the division was far from fully ready for renewed action when the Russians launched their anticipated summer offensive on 22 June, the third anniversary of the start of Operation 'Barbarossa'.

General histories by Western historians often neglect this campaign, mostly because they are focused in on D-Day and the battle to break out of the Normandy beach–head, but also because eastern Europe is less familiar and events there assumed to be of less interest to readers, but in fact the Red Army could have won the war entirely on its own by this time. If the Western Allies tied down German forces in France which could otherwise have been deployed in the east, the reverse of that coin is even more true. Had Stalin accepted Hitler's peace initiative in the early summer of 1943 — before Kursk — and permitted German occupation of European Russia west of the Dnieper, the Allies would not just have been thrown out of Italy but would never have secured a toehold in France. Such are the 'What ifs?' of history!

As it was, even before the Soviet summer offensive began, the Crimea had been recaptured and some 200,000 Germans had been killed or captured by the time of the fall of Sevastopol on 9 May. Moreover, in the north — where III (Germanische) SS Korps, now comprising *Nordland* and *Nederland*, was operating — the Russians had completed the relief of Leningrad and driven the Germans back into Latvia and Estonia, where the 15th and 19th Latvian and 20th Estonian Divisions of VI SS Korps were still fighting tenaciously on the Narva Front, between the Gulf of Finland and Lake Peipus. (The other Waffen-SS division whose operations have not already been described, *Nord*, was still fighting on the Finnish Front, having been returned to action in August 1942 after its ignominious rout at Salla the previous year. It would remain until September 1944 when it was moved west to Norway after Finland agreed a separate armistice with Russia. Later, greatly understrength and redesignated a *Kampfgruppe*, it would return to Germany via Denmark and see some action in the Ardennes and the Saar regions, finally surrendering to American forces in Bavaria at the end of the war.)

The German high command expected that the summer offensive would again fall upon Army Group South, now renamed Army Group North Ukraine, but instead the first blow fell against Field Marshal Ernst Busch's Army Group Centre (Busch having replaced Kluge in October 1943 when the latter was seriously injured in a car crash). The operation, codenamed 'Bagration' after the great General who had done so much to defeat Napoleon in 1812–14, involved larger forces than the Wehrmacht had deployed for the start of Operation 'Barbarossa'. In total, the Soviet armed forces had over six million men facing 2¼ million Axis troops, but more significantly they had 2¼ million men, 4,000 tanks and 28,600 guns* facing Army Group Centre's 300-mile front while Busch could only muster 700,000 men, 900 tanks and 10,000 guns. He *should* have had more, but one of Model's first acts as commander of Army Group North Ukraine had actually been to persuade Hitler to transfer LVI Panzer Korps from Busch's to his own command. Moreover, many of the Russian tanks were uprated T–34s with 85 instead of 76 mm guns or the new IS–2s with 122 mm weapons which outclassed even the Tiger, while the Soviet air force had a massive superiority of 5,300 aircraft to the Luftwaffe's mere 1,300 because Göring had transferred large numbers to France and Germany after D-Day.

Busch had pleaded with Hitler to permit a strategic withdrawal behind the River Beresina to shorten his lines but, predictably, the Führer would hear nothing of it and instead designated the towns of Vitebsk, Orsha, Mogilev and Bobruisk as 'fortified centres' which were to be held at all costs. The costs, indeed, would be high.

The sledgehammer fell during the night of 22/23 June after a mammoth aerial attack which destroyed hundreds of German aircraft on the ground and an artillery barrage which rocked the earth. The defenders were helpless to withstand the onslaught and the Russians surged forward, advancing an average of 25 miles in the first two days and surrounding LIII Korps of Third Panzer Army at Vitebsk on 25 June. A breakout attempt proved futile and the Korps commander surrendered the survivors of his 35,000 men on 27 June, the same day that Orsha also fell. To the south of Vitebsk, Fourth Army's XXXIX Panzer Korps — 'Panzer' in name only, because it did not have a single operational tank! — had already been overrun and annihilated east of Mogilev, and the same fate befell Ninth Army's XLI Panzer Korps. Bobruisk fell on the 29th leaving XXXV Korps also surrounded and abandoned to its fate because there were no reserves for a relief attempt. Busch had ordered a general retreat behind the Beresina on 28 June but it was already too late. Within a week Army Group Centre had lost the best part of 28 divisions — 300–350,000 men — as well as nearly a third of its tanks and some 1,500 guns. The front was wide open and the triumphant Red Army surged into Poland.

Hitler sacked Busch on 28 June and gave Model command of Army Group Centre as well as his existing forces, which was harsh on Busch but a sensible — even though ultimately futile — move, because it centralized the command structure on the threatened sectors. This was just as well, for on 13 July Koniev threw his 1st Ukrainian Front against Army Group North Ukraine. (This was actually the third of the Russian summer

---

* 24,400 according to some sources.

Above Wiking *Division Panther in the summer of 1944.*

Below *Panther and infantry of the* Wiking *Division photographed at approximately the same time.*

SS troops in Warsaw.

assaults, for on 4 July Army Group North had also come under attack and was being driven back through the Baltic States. On 10 July Model had asked Hitler to withdraw Army Group Centre's northern flank, but the Führer refused.) Regardless, as in the centre, Model's southern forces were thrown back rapidly, eight divisions being surrounded and captured east of Lvov, which fell on 27 July. Pinsk had already fallen on 14 July and Lublin on 23 July, and by the end of the month the Russians were across the Vistula and approaching Warsaw.

Totenkopf had arrived in Poland on 7 July and been entrusted with the defence of Grodno, but faced with odds of 7:1 in men and 10:1 in tanks was forced to fall back on 18 July, joining the general westward rush. Ten days later the division held open the Warsaw Highway over the Vistula at Siedlce, assisted by the Luftwaffe's crack *Herman Göring* Division, allowing the last German troops capable of retreating to escape. At the beginning of August *Totenkopf* was joined by *Wiking*, rested and back to nearly full strength after its escape from Cherkassy, in a new IV SS Panzer Korps under Herbert Gille. They did not take part in the ruthless crushing of the Warsaw uprising, when the Polish 'Home Army' attempted to throw the Germans out of the city in anticipation of the early arrival of the Red Army.

This ghastly task was entrusted, as we have seen, to the police and the Dirlewanger and Kaminski Brigades.* Instead, the two SS divisions together with *Herman Göring* and the 4th and 19th Panzer Divisions actually counter-attacked thirty miles north-east of Warsaw, retaking Praga and virtually destroying the Soviet Second Tank Army.

The Soviet offensive into Poland now ran out of steam, the troops too exhausted and the vehicles too badly in need of maintenance and repair to advance any further until the gains of the previous weeks had been consolidated and supply lines shortened. So, before looking at the Soviet advances in the Balkans and on the Baltic Front, and at the final winter offensive which would take them to Berlin, it is appropriate to examine the dramatic events which had been taking place in France.

* * *

As spring turned into summer in that fateful year of 1944, the German high command had three principal worries. One was obviously the virtual collapse of the Eastern Front. The second was the accumulative effect that Allied strategic bombing was having on German industry and civilian morale, the US Army Air Force pounding the cities by day while the Royal Air Force came over night after night. And the third was where the long-expected Allied amphibious landing would take place. Would it be from Egypt into Greece or from southern Italy into Yugoslavia to link up with the Red Army? Would it be from Italy into southern France? Would it be from Scotland into Norway and thence southward down through Denmark into Germany itself? Or would it be on the Channel coast, and if so, where? All were possibilities and Allied plans existed for each, but the Channel coast of France was in fact the chosen target.

The Germans realized this probability, but had to keep divisions stationed elsewhere in case they were wrong: 12 in Norway and 21 in the Balkans, as well as a home reserve of nine, all of which could have been better deployed. Allied deception methods strongly pointed to the Pas de Calais as the most probable landing area, but other possibilities were Normandy or even a left hook around the Brittany peninsula on to the Biscay coast between St Nazaire and Bordeaux. This meant that Field

---

* An estimated 200,000 Poles died between the beginning of August and the end of organized resistance on 2 October. The Russians permitted only one airlift of supplies to the Home Army during this period, on 18 September, but of 1,284 parachute containers dropped, 1,056 fell into German hands. The reasons why the Red Army did not rush to the relief of Warsaw have been endlessly debated. In the wake of German revelations about the massacre of 4,100 Polish officers by the Russians, whose graves were uncovered in Katyn Wood in April 1943, Western historians have generally taken the line that it suited Stalin to have the Germans kill the Poles rather than have to get the Red Army to do it later. Soviet historians, on the other hand, have argued that it was the Red Army's exhaustion and the strength of the defence put up by *Wiking* and *Totenkopf* in particular, which prevented their intervention in the massacre. The former is still the most likely explanation in my own opinion.

Tiger Is of the 3rd Company, sSSPzAbt 101, on their way to the Normandy front.

Marshal Gerd von Rundstedt's 58 divisions* were thinly spread all the way from the Hook of Holland to the Spanish border, and along the Mediterranean coast from Perpignan to Nice, with the greatest concentration between Zeebrugge and Le Havre. Of those divisions, the Waffen-SS were to play a part in the forthcoming campaign out of all proportion to their numbers.

The actual German forces in France and the Low Countries on D-Day comprised 31 infantry, two parachute, six Panzer and two training divisions in Field Marshal Erwin Rommel's Army Group B north of the Loire, including the Leibstandarte and *Hitler Jugend*; and eight infantry, three Panzer, one Panzergrenadier and five training divisions in General Johannes Blaskowitz's Army Group G south of the Loire, including *Das Reich* and *Götz von Berlichingen*.

The dispositions behind the 'Atlantic Wall' which Rommel had been busily reinforcing since November 1943 reflected both the success of the Allied deception measures and disagreements between the German Generals. Rommel had wanted to concentrate the Panzer divisions close to the coast because he rightly feared that Allied aerial superiority would render mobile operations impossible by day. Gerd von Rundstedt, however, as C-in-C West, insisted that the Panzer divisions be held back

* There were in fact 60 divisions in total but two do not count: the 40,000-strong 319th Infantry Division which formed the Channel Islands' garrison and the 19th Panzer Division which was recuperating in Holland after being severely mauled in Russia.

from the coast to act as a mobile reserve which could counter-attack when the direction of the main Allied thrust was known. He was also worried about the effect of Allied naval bombardment on his tanks and was supported in these views by both the commander of Panzergruppe West, General Freiherr Geyr von Schweppenburg, and by the Inspector-General of Armoured Forces, Heinz Guderian.

The result of all this was to create confusion and delay, with resultant heavy casualties, when the first 50,000 of an eventual two million Allied soldiers began pouring ashore on 6 June. Closest of the Panzer divisions to the Normandy beaches were the 12th SS Panzer Division *Hitler Jugend*, Panzer Lehr and the 21st Panzer Division. *Hitler Jugend* formed part of I SS Panzer Korps under 'Sepp' Dietrich, the other components being the Leibstandarte, now commanded by Brigadeführer Theodor Wisch,* and the 101st *schwere SS Panzer Abteilung* (Heavy SS Tank Battalion); the Leibstandarte was at Beverloo in Belgium and the 101st sSSPzABT near Beauvais. The 17th SS Panzergrenadier Division *Götz von Berlichingen* was at Bayonne, *Das Reich* at Toulouse and the 102nd sSSPzABT was in Holland. Of the Army Panzer divisions, the 2nd was north-east of Dieppe, the 116th outside Paris north of the Seine, the 11th right down near Bordeaux and the 9th even further away at Nîmes. The latter would not be able to join in the fight until August! In addition the Army had its own heavy tank battalion, the 503rd, which was training up in Thuringia with brand-new Tiger IIs armed with high-velocity 8.8 cm guns.

Hitler Jugend was the first SS division on the scene on 7 June, its leading elements arriving late in the afternoon to join the 21st Panzer Division which had halted Montgomery's drive on Caen the previous day even though it had been unable to push the British I Corps back to its beach, codename 'Sword'. Despite the fact that only one of the SS division's Panzer battalions was present, the second being stranded for lack of petrol north of the River Orne, they knocked out 28 tanks of the Canadian I Corps advancing from 'Juno' beach for the loss of only two of their own destroyed and four damaged during a bitter battle around Carpiquet airfield. The young soldiers of the *Hitler Jugend*, commanded by Brigadeführer Fritz Witt, had proved their worth in their first battle.

The Caen perimeter formed the eastern shoulder of the Allied beach-head and it was Montgomery's intention to suck the three German Panzer divisions known to be in the area into a battle of attrition so as to allow the America armour to exploit the more open countryside further west around St Lô as well as into the Cotentin peninsula, the early capture of the major port of Cherbourg being vital to the Allied build-up.

Panzer Lehr was delayed in its approach to Caen by American and British fighter-bombers and did not arrive until 8 June, positioning itself on the left flank of *Hitler Jugend*. The plan was to advance on the axis of the N13 road towards Bayeux, which was already in Allied hands, and seal off the

---

* One of the youngest divisional commanders ever, Wisch was only 37 at the time and already held the Knights Cross with Oakleaves and Swords.

Anglo-Canadian beachheads. Panzer Lehr made good progress on 9 June and got to within three miles of Bayeux, but threatened with an Allied outflanking drive was forced to withdraw. Montgomery was pressing aggressively forward west of Caen and after heavy fighting around Tilly and Lingèvres, Panzer Lehr found itself in dire straits because of the threat from 7th Armoured Division which reached Villers Bocage on 13 June. Succour came from a most unexpected source in what has subsequently become the most famous individual tank engagement of the war...

Obersturmführer Michael Wittmann was curious. With 119 'kills' behind him in Russia, the blond-haired 30-year-old veteran was already the war's top tank ace, but he had never fought the British or Americans. When the 101st sSSPzAbt arrived in the Caen area on 12 June after a hazardous journey, he was commander of the battalion's 2nd Company of Tiger tanks, and immediately wanted to see for himself what sort of a mess the Army's elite Panzer Lehr Division had got itself into. First thing on the morning of 13 June*, he set out with four Tigers and a PzKpfw IV to reconnoitre. Bypassing a column of 7th Armoured Division tanks ('A' Squadron, 22nd Armoured Brigade) which had paused alongside a

---

* Coincidentally, the day the first V1 flying bomb landed in England.

A Tiger I of sSSPzAbt 101 driving through Morgny, near Rouen, on its way to the Caen sector.

hedgerow to brew tea and did not notice them, Wittmann took his own Tiger (believed to have had the turret number 200) into the village of Villers Bocage itself, where he promptly knocked out three of 22nd Armoured Brigade's headquarters Cromwell tanks; a fourth quickly reversed unnoticed out of sight and proceeded to stalk him.

Round the corner at the bottom of the hill Wittmann ran headlong into 'B' Squadron and, after an exchange of shots during which the Tiger was hit but not incapacitated, he ordered his driver to reverse into a side road and return up the hill. Here he came face to face with the fourth HQ Cromwell, which scored two hits before being itself knocked out by the Tiger's 8.8 cm gun. Wittmann then rejoined his other four tanks and, after replenishing his own ammunition from some of theirs, led two of the Tigers and the PzKpfw IV into an attack against the unsuspecting 'A' Squadron. A wood concealed their approach and Wittmann's tanks rapidly knocked out the leading and rearmost of the squadron's tanks, blocking their exits from the narrow lane, then systematically destroyed the other 23, along with a variety of half-tracks and Bren Gun Carriers.

Now, though, Wittmann overplayed his hand. He led his small command back into Villers Bocage, where 'B' Squadron had deployed its tanks and a 6 pr anti-tank gun in ambush positions on the left side of the road. As the German tanks passed, they were knocked out one by one by point-blank shots from the sides and rear, where their armour was thinnest. The surviving crew members (including Wittmann) leapt out of their stricken vehicles and, dodging through the rubble of the heavily bombed village, made their escape.

In the overall context of the war it had been a very minor action, but it prevented 7th Armoured from encircling Panzer Lehr, whose grateful divisional commander* recommended Wittmann for the Swords to go with his Knights Cross with Oakleaves. He was also promoted and given command of the battalion, but was killed on 8 August at Gaumesnil when his new Tiger (number 007!) was surrounded by five British M4 Shermans. Hauptsturmführer Michael Wittmann's final score was 138 enemy tanks destroyed. He was buried in a communal grave until 1983 when his body was disinterred and given a proper funeral in the German military cemetery at La Cambe.

Meanwhile, further German Panzer reinforcements were slowly struggling to the front, harassed during the day by Allied fighter-bombers and slowed at night by the havoc which bombing and the efforts of the French Resistance wreaked on the railway lines and rolling stock. First was Brigadeführer Werner Ostendorff's 17th SS Panzergrenadier Division *Götz von Berlichingen* which had arrived in the Carentan sector facing the Americans from 'Utah' and 'Omaha' beaches during the night of 10/11 June. Two days later it made a determined effort to retake the town but was eventually repulsed. The Army's 2nd Panzer Division began to arrive after a tortuous journey to reinforce Panzer Lehr's left flank on the same day as

* Lieutenant-General Fritz Bayerlein, Rommel's former Chief-of-Staff in Africa.

Tiger IIs of sPzAbt 503 hide from Allied fighter-bombers in a wood while British prisoners push a wheelbarrow.

Wittmann's exploit, but it was to be a further five days before their tanks reached the scene. Next was the 503rd sPzAbt with its Tiger IIs on 7 July, followed by the Leibstandarte and the 102nd sSSPzAbt on the 9th. The latter, commanded by Obersturmbannführer Hans Weiss, formed part of the new II SS Panzer Korps under Brigadeführer Wilhelm Bittrich, CO of the 9th SS Panzer Division *Hohenstaufen*. Hastily recalled from the Eastern Front alongside Brigadeführer Lothar Debes's 10th SS Panzer Division *Frundsberg*, *Hohenstaufen* had endured a nightmare journey from Poland and only arrived on 25 June, the day before Montgomery launched his next major attack. The 116th 'Greyhound' Panzer Division was held in reserve until late July and 9th Panzer did not complete re-equipping in the south of France until 27 June, arriving in Normandy on 6 August.

The 2nd SS Panzer Division *Das Reich* unfortunately deserves special attention here.

The moment news of the Allied landings in Normandy hit their eagerly awaiting ears, thousands of Frenchmen who had been storing arms, ammunition and explosives against the day leapt into action. Their intention was to cause as much behind-the-lines disruption and to kill as many Germans as they could. German military authorities had been well aware of this possibility and, coincidentally, on the very day before D-Day, the *Das Reich*'s own commander, Brigadeführer Heinz Lammerding, had sent in a memo — which was endorsed by Army Group G's General Blaskowitz — recommending that three French civilians should be hanged in reprisal for every German soldier wounded by the Maquis and 10 for every one killed. The scene was therefore set for the atrocities which followed.

The Maquis hounded the SS division at every stage of their long march, which began on 8 June, snipers and tiny assault groups armed with Bren light machine-guns and Sten sub-machine-guns as well as grenades and bazookas supplied by SOE opening fire at the slowly moving target of some 15,000 men and 1,400 vehicles at each and every opportunity. The division felt the attacks like a man feels the bites of mosquitoes: individually, they were insignificant, but as they built up tempers frayed and judgements became warped by the incessant pinpricks, by the summer heat and the lack of a 'proper' enemy who could be brought to battle.

The division's reconnaissance battalion — now commanded by Sturmbannführer Heinrich Wulf since the hero of Belgrade, Fritz Klingenberg, had gone on to an instructor's role at Bad Tölz* — was assigned a rescue mission on 9 June. The German garrison at Tulle had been practically overwhelmed by the Maquis and the survivors — all elderly reservists — were pinned down in a factory and adjoining school. The SS battalion rapidly cleared the village of the ill-trained Maquisards, suffering only three men killed. By the following morning, though, they realized that the French had slaughtered 139 men from the village garrison, 40 of whose bodies had been mutilated. It was announced that 120 Maquisards would be hanged in reprisal. The 3,000 villagers were rounded up and searched. Most were quickly dismissed, to their great relief, and in the end a group of 400 trembling suspects remained. The hangings began in the afternoon, and 99 men were killed before the executions were inexplicably called off. Only two of the dead were actually in the Resistance.

The march of *Das Reich* to Normandy was constantly hampered by the need to clear towns and villages on its route of Resistance fighters, and the SS soldiers soon found it was dangerous to go out alone at night. One specific incident produced the next and most horrifying massacre. On the evening of 9 June Sturmbannführer Helmut Kämpfe, popular CO of the 3rd Battalion, Regiment *Der Führer*, was driving back to his headquarters when his car was surrounded by a group of armed men and he was led away into the gathering dusk, never to be seen again. His abandoned car was discovered and a futile search instituted.

On the morning of 10 June Sturmbannführer Otto Dickmann, CO of the 1st Battalion, arrived at regimental headquarters in Limoges in a state of high excitement because villagers in St Junien had told him of a German officer being held prisoner by the Maquis in Oradour-sur-Glane. Dickmann was convinced it must be Kämpfe, who was a close friend, and received permission to investigate. He took the 120 men of his 3rd Company and drove off. Arriving early afternoon in the sleepy little village, Dickmann's men wasted no time in racing from house to house, driving

* In January 1945 Standartenführer Klingenberg became the penultimate commander of *Götz von Berlichingen* and was killed in action on 22 March.

the inhabitants into the Champ de Faire ('fairground'). There was no sign of Kampfe. The women and children were herded into the church and some of the men thrust into barns and garages. Then the shooting began. Machine-guns poured fire into the men sitting in the field while other soldiers shot those in the buildings before setting fire to them. It was the same story in the church. A total of 648 people perished (some sources say 642). There were a few lucky survivors, such as three Jewish girls who had stayed in hiding while the SS searched the buildings. When the shooting started, they fled, only to bump straight into an SS Private. This decent man gestured for them to run. Other villagers returning to Oradour were intercepted by a patrol; they too were told to scatter and hide. Only one woman escaped from the church, but a few men managed to hide themselves under the piles of other bodies and likewise escaped after Dickmann's men had gone. *

The savagery of Dickmann's action — for which he was censured but not court martialled as some of his superiors requested — caused the Resistance to pull in their horns: if reprisals were going to be on this scale, then killing a few German soldiers was not worth the candle. Consequently there were few other incidents involving the Maquis, and the division began to arrive in Normandy on 15 June, being positioned on the St Lô front facing the Americans.

Now, on 26 June, the day before the last defenders surrendered in Cherbourg, Montgomery launched a new offensive in the Caen sector, codenamed 'Epsom'. The objective of this was a hill, simply known as 'Hill 112' on the maps, lying to the south-west of Caen near Baron in between the rivers Odon and Orne, which dominated the surrounding countryside. Because of the dense hedgerows and narrow lanes, Montgomery used fresh infantry from the 15th and 43rd Divisions to precede 11th Armoured Division's tanks, which made good progress to begin with and thoroughly alarmed 'Sepp' Dietrich, who demanded that Rommel release additional reserves to stem the tide. With reluctance, the Field Marshal committed II SS Panzer Korps to the battle.

The British attack, supported by wave after wave of aircraft and shells from Royal Navy warships, was still only contained with difficulty, and over a hundred tanks were lost in the battle which raged until 1 July. By this time, though, the writing was very definitely on the wall. 'What shall we do? What shall we do?', moaned Field Marshal Wilhelm Keitel over the telephone to von Rundstedt. 'Make peace†, you fools!', the old soldier replied. Next day he was dismissed and replaced by Field Marshal Günther von Kluge. Other changes included the replacement of Freiherr Geyr von

---

* Dickmann was killed by a shell splinter on 30 June so never stood trial, but 21 of his men were found and indicted; two were hanged and the remainder given stiff prison sentences. Another 42 were sentenced to death in their absence but have not been brought to justice so far, to my knowledge.

† 'End the war' according to some sources, but the sense is the same!

Tank commander wearing the mottle camouflage tanker's jacket which was unique to the Waffen-SS.

Schweppenburg as commander of Panzergruppe West by General Heinrich Eberbach, and the appointment of Obergruppenführer Paul Hausser as commander of Seventh Army when General Friedrich Dollmann died of a heart attack.

Over the following days the Allies succeeded in capturing half of Carpiquet airfield at long last, despite the fierce resistance of *Hitler Jugend*, and by 8 July most of Caen was also in their hands after massive bombing raids had almost totally reduced the city to rubble. Hill 112 finally fell on 11 July. This set the stage for Montgomery's next major offensive codenamed 'Goodwood', to break the stalemate around Caen, on 18 July — the same day the Americans took St Lô. By chance, Rommel had been badly injured during an Allied fighter attack the previous day, leaving Kluge in personal charge of Army Group B as well as overall command in France, and two days later the whole fabric of Nazi Germany would be rocked by the so nearly successful attempt on Hitler's life when Colonel Claus von Stauffenberg left a bomb under the table in the Führer's bunker.

For 'Goodwood', Montgomery used the Guards, 7th and 11th Armoured Divisions, all veteran formations; they were opposed by the Leibstandarte, *Hitler Jugend* and 21st Panzer Division, all of which had been seriously weakened over the last month but were still adversaries to be reckoned with. (German casualties in Normandy up to this point totalled 97,000 while replacements only amounted to 6,000; similarly, 225 tanks had been destroyed and only 17 new ones received.) Montgomery's attack was preceded by the predictable heavy bombing raid by over 2,000 aircraft and a massive artillery bombardment which inflicted serious damage, but the Panzers held on by the skin of their teeth although finally having to evacuate Caen. It seemed to many, especially those in the Allied front line, as though 'Monty' had underestimated the strength of the opposition, for he certainly had not achieved the anticipated breakthrough, but in fact the operation had been deliberately designed to suck the Panzer divisions into the Caen sector to make way for General Omar Bradley's breakout thrust from St Lô towards Avranches.

Lacking Rommel's perspicacity, Kluge responded just as Montgomery had hoped and denuded his eastern perimeter of all its armour but for *Das Reich, Götz von Berlichingen* and Panzer Lehr (which by this time were mere shadows of their former selves), meaning that Hausser could muster fewer than 200 tanks to contain the American onslaught. The remaining divisions in Panzer Group West — now retitled Fifth Panzer Army and commanded temporarily by 'Sepp' Dietrich — were all assigned to the Caen front. The fact that two Waffen-SS Generals were, in effect, now in charge of the tactical situation in Normandy reflects both Hitler's faith in Himmler's creation and his steadily growing disillusionment with his regular Army Generals, especially after the 20 July bomb plot.*

Bradley's breakout, scheduled to have begun on 19 July, was delayed until 25 July by bad weather which would have rendered proper aerial support impossible, and by this time the Allies realized that it was local air supremacy over the battlefield which was slowly winning the war for them. Operation 'Cobra', as it was codenamed, was ushered in by a force of nearly 3,000 aircraft which dropped over 4,000 tons of bombs (some of them falling on the American lines because the opposing forces were so closely engaged in the dense Normandy hedgerows) and reduced Panzer Lehr to virtually nothing; at one point only seven tanks remained in running order and it took all the engineers' work over the next two days to raise that to 28. German survivors have said that after the bombing the landscape looked like the face of the Moon, and that the craters were more of a hindrance to the advancing Americans than were their own efforts at defence.

By 28 July Hausser's Seventh Army had essentially ceased to exist; the whole of the west Normandy flank was wide open and on the evening of

---

* Rommel and Kluge were both implicated although their 'sins' were more of omission than commission. Rommel, as is well known, was given the choice of voluntarily swallowing poison or standing trial and seeing his family in a concentration camp. Knowing his life was forfeit in either case, he took the former course on 14 October and was buried with hero's honours. Kluge preceded him, taking cyanide on 19 August after his failure to contain the Allied breakout and his replacement in command by Walter Model — the 'fireman' of the Eastern Front — on 17 August.

the 30th Avranches was cleared by the US 4th Armored Division. Never one to hesitate, General George S. Patton, Jr, whose Third Army was now operational, fanned his forces out, some into Brittany, some more directly southwards, and some east alongside First Army to hammer the divisions still fighting around Caen against the Anglo-Canadian anvil. Montgomery had launched the second stage of 'Goodwood' on the 30th, designed to prevent Kluge sending reinforcements to Hausser, but Hitler had other ideas and ordered a mass Panzer attack in the direction of Arromanches through Mortain to seal the gap in the lines and cut off the US Third Army. Kluge hardly had the strength left to 'mass' anything and the abortive counter-attack on 8 August was launched with a mere 185 tanks from the Leibstandarte, *Das Reich* and the 2nd and 116th Panzer Divisions. Although *Das Reich* succeeded in recapturing Mortain, the operation was a fiasco and within days the Germans were back where they had started. Meanwhile, in the east the British and Canadians had finally captured Villers Bocage.

This marked the beginning of what has entered history as the battle of Falaise. Squeezed by the Second British and First Canadian Armies from the north and the First and Third American Armies swinging round into their rear from the south-west, the remnants of the proud Waffen-SS and Army Panzer divisions found themselves trapped in a steadily contracting pocket. The Allied bombers and rocket-firing fighters had a field day against such a concentrated target, from which the only exit was the rapidly shrinking 'neck' between Falaise and Argentan. It was only the heroic efforts of *Hitler Jugend*, plus a counter-attack by *Das Reich* and *Hohenstaufen* (which had escaped earlier), which allowed so many men and vehicles to get out of the trap. Even so, of approximately 100,000 soldiers in Fifth Panzer and Seventh Armies only some 40,000 managed to escape before the jaws clamped shut on 21 August, by which time Allied troops had reached the River Seine and were pressing on towards Paris, which they reached on 24 August. The Germans also had another threat to contend with, for on 15 August American and Free French troops had landed on the Mediterranean coast of southern France and Blaskowitz's weak Army Group G was in full — albeit controlled — retreat.

The Leibstandarte was pulled back via Belgium to the Aachen area, *Das Reich* to the Schnee-Eifel, *Hohenstaufen* and *Frundsberg* to Arnhem, *Hitler Jugend* back east of the River Maas and *Götz von Berlichingen* to Metz. The two heavy tank battalions were also withdrawn for rest and refit and redesignated 501st and 502nd *schwere SS Panzer Abteilungen*, both re-equipped with Tiger IIs. None of the SS formations was heavily involved in fighting during the long retreat across France, being too bably mauled to be effective, but *Hohenstaufen* and *Frundsberg* were to see action again under rather unexpected circumstances within a month.

The speed of the German collapse in France came as a surprise to the Allies and they tumbled forward into a virtual vacuum, delayed only by weak battlegroups and rapidly outrunning their supply lines. The Germans abandoned Belgium, Brussels being liberated on 3 September and the last German troops escaping to the northern bank of the River Scheldt at Antwerp on 4 September. At this point Hitler recalled von Rundstedt to take over as C-in-C West again, retaining Model as commander of Army Group B, while Blaskowitz was replaced by Major-General Hermann Balck.

Montgomery was a very orthodox soldier, as can be seen in his conduct of the battles of El Alamein and Caen, so it is somewhat surprising that his next plan showed something of the genius of a Manstein and perhaps even more surprising that, after having been refused earlier, he persuaded Eisenhower to accept it on 10 September. It was obvious that the Germans would oppose a crossing of the Rhine with all their strength, so it would be greatly to the Allied advantage if a bridgehead could be established across the river while they were still disorganized and demoralized after their defeat in France. To this end Montgomery proposed that airborne forces should capture key bridges over the Rivers Aa, Dommel and the Wilhelmina and Zuid Willemsvaart Canals at Eindhoven, over the Rivers Maas, Waal and the Maas-Waal Canal at Grave and Nijemegen and over the lower Rhine at Arnhem. This would lay a 'carpet' for General Sir Brian Horrocks's XXX Corps to lead Second Army's way straight across Holland and open the path eastward into the north German plain and the industrial Ruhr, simultaneously cutting off those German troops still in western Holland.

The operation, codenamed 'Market Garden', began after a hectic six days' preparation on Sunday, 17 September, and to begin with seemed to be going well. The US 101st Airborne Division dropped at Eindhoven at 13:00 hours and rapidly secured its objectives, while Horrocks's Corps, spearheaded by the Guards Armoured Division, punched through General Kurt Student's newly formed First Parachute Army and raced to join them. Similarly, the US 82nd Airborne Division landed successfully south of Nijmegen and quickly secured the bridge over the Maas at Grave but was unable to take that over the Waal, which was heavily defended. It was at this point that things started going wrong. At Arnhem they never went right, for not only had Allied intelligence failed to report the presence of Bittrich's II SS Panzer Korps north-east of the town, but it also missed the presence of Model's own headquarters in the western suburb of Oosterbeek. Thanks to the Field Marshal's on the spot presence, the German response was immediate and the British 1st Airborne Division soon found itself in grave difficulties.

Due to the nature of the terrain the paras had to be dropped up to eight miles from the bridge which was their objective; they had to go in in separate waves instead of a single drop because of the shortage of aircraft and because getting the American divisions to their own objectives took priority, which resulted in their being scattered rather than concentrated; they found themselves up against veteran SS Panzertruppen who both outnumbered them and were better equipped with tanks and other heavy

SS and Army troops with a StuG III and captured British paras during the fierce battle around Arnhem.

weapons; and, forced to proceed along a single highway, blocked at Nijmegen, Horrocks was unable to push XXX Corps through to them in the planned two to four days. His tanks could not move off the elevated road because of the surrounding dikes and ditches.

Realizing the situation within hours of the first landings, Model (who is portrayed very unfairly in the film *A Bridge Too Far*) ordered Bittrich to use *Hohenstaufen* to hold off and eventually virtually annihilate the British paras at Arnhem, sending *Frundsberg* pell-mell down the road to reinforce the troops in Nijmegen. Here, they held out until 20 September when the combined might of XXX Corps and the 82nd Airborne finally forced a passage, but this was enough to seal the fate of the troops in and around Arnhem. Only the 2nd Battalion under Lieutenant-Colonel John Frost had actually reached the bridge itself, and they were slowly worn down until forced to surrender. The remainder of the division found itself compressed in a pocket outside the town and a relief attempt by the Independent Polish Parachute Brigade failed on 22 September. Just under a third of the 10,000 involved managed to escape across the Rhine over 25–27 September to rejoin the Allied lines; over 1,200 were killed and most of the remainder entered captivity, although a few hid out in Dutch houses. Total Anglo-American and Polish casualties were over 7,000 compared to 1,100 Germans killed and about twice that number wounded. Montgomery's gamble had failed and the Allies would not now cross the Rhine until 7 March 1945, while Arnhem itself would not be liberated until 15 April.

After describing some of the earlier atrocities, it is worth recording here that Bittrich and most of his men behaved correctly and with chivalry throughout the bitter struggle for the bridgehead, offering their captives brandy, chocolate and cigarettes and at one point agreeing to a ceasefire so the badly wounded among the paras could be taken to Dutch and German hospitals for proper treatment.

*   *   *

By the time of the battle of Arnhem, the Eastern Front was in a state of chaos. Russian troops reached the Bulgarian frontier on 1 September; on 2 September Finland broke off diplomatic relations with Germany and demanded the withdrawal of all German troops; on 6 September Soviet troops in Romania reached the Yugoslav frontier and on 8 September Bulgaria joined Romania in declaring war on Germany; on 16 September the Red Army entered Sofia; four days later Talinn, capital of Estonia, also fell, and on 23 September Russian troops arrived on the Hungarian border. Hungary was the strongest of Germany's Eastern Front allies, and her collapse would drastically weaken the German position. To prevent this, German troops had already occupied the country on 19 March. Now

SS paratroops on the Eastern Front late in 1944.

Hitler discovered that the Regent, Admiral Miklós Horthy, was in secret negotiations with the Russians.

The Führer entrusted his favourite SS commando, Sturmbannführer Otto Skorzeny, with a top secret mission: kidnap the Regent's son, Nikolaus, to force Horthy to stay in the war. The tall, scar-faced officer visited Budapest disguised as a tourist and laid his plans carefully. On 15 October he struck, his men seizing the unsuspecting Nikolaus after a short gun battle with his guards, rolling him in a carpet and driving him to the airport. It was too late: at 14:00 on the same day Admiral Horthy announced over the radio that Germany had lost the war and that he was seeking armistice terms.

At dawn the following morning Skorzeny bluffed his way into Castle Hill and led his troops in an assault on the Regent's Palace, which was seized with only 26 German and Hungarian dead. Horthy escaped but announced his abdication later in the day; he was flown to Germany and placed under house arrest for the remainder of the war. A new puppet government was formed under the Hungarian Nazi leader Ferenc Szalasy which promptly repudiated the armistice.

Skorzeny's next exploit took place under totally different circumstances, during what has entered history as 'the Battle of the Bulge'.

After Arnhem, the war on the Western Front entered a relatively quiet phase, a phase of consolidation and retrenchment rather than major operations for both sides. The Allies tightened their hold on the steadily shrinking German perimeter — for the whole of Nazi territory was now one vast 'pocket' without a bolthole — while Himmler, entrusted with charge of the 'Replacement Army', resorted to dragging every reasonably able-bodied man from 16-year-olds to grandfathers into uniform. This was, as Propaganda Minister Josef Göbbels constantly reminded the German population, now 'total war'.

While von Rundstedt, Model, Balck and Student succeeded in stalling the Western Allies at Aachen, Antwerp and Metz* during October and November, Hitler and Himmler were busily rebuilding the Panzer divisions for the grandiose counter-offensive the Führer had begun planning as early as August. Codenamed *Wacht am Rhein* ('Watch on the Rhine'), the operation was designed to sweep through the Ardennes just as the Panzer divisions had done in 1940, recross the River Meuse and thrust through to Antwerp. Quite what this would have accomplished even if it had succeeded is difficult to imagine. Hitler believed that he would cut off the Canadian First, British Second and American First and Ninth Armies in northern Belgium and Holland, after which he would be able to use the V1s and V2s to secure a ceasefire in the west and transfer his forces to drive back the Russians. This was a pipedream from beginning to end, as Rundstedt and Model fully realized. It would be a miracle if they managed to get across the Meuse! The roads through the Ardennes did not run in

---

* Where *Götz von Berlichingen* was reduced from 16,000 to only 4,000 men and a mere *four* tanks.

the right direction and, being steep, winding and narrow, would be even more impassable in the snow and ice than in the summer. Moreover, there was not enough fuel for a sustained drive. These objections, Hitler countered, were actually advantages, for the Allies would be even less likely to expect an attack in this sector, and as for petrol, well, the Americans had plenty which could be captured, did they not? The Field Marshals dutifully went away to do as they were told, for after the bomb plot no one dared cross the maniacal puppeteer in Berlin. Even 'Sepp' Dietrich, newly appointed CO of Sixth SS Panzer Army for the attack, commented with raw peasant humour that if ever he wanted to get shot, opposing his Führer was the best way to go about it.

Hitler and Himmler achieved miracles between 16 September — the day formal planning for the offensive began — and 16 December, when it started. No fewer than 18 new or reconstituted divisions were assembled for operations in the west in just over two months. The preparations were made under the tightest security and the bulk of the forces assembled for the attack were gathered together in the Saar and Aachen sectors, which was where the Allies would logically expect the majority of reserves to be sent. False radio traffic even deceived the 'Ultra' boffins so that when the blow fell it came as a complete surprise.

Dietrich's Sixth SS Panzer Army on the right flank consisted of four veteran Panzer divisions, the Leibstandarte, *Das Reich, Hohenstaufen* and *Hitler Jugend* plus elements from others — particularly ethnic Belgians and Dutchmen who could, it was hoped, help in smoothing the passage and in occupation duties; together with the 3rd Parachute and 12th, 272nd, 277th and 326th Volksgrenadier Divisions, the latter all formed by Himmler from veteran cadres of previous infantry divisions, not the untrained 'Johnnie-come-latelies' the word 'Volksgrenadier' often suggests.

To Dietrich's left was Fifth Panzer Army commanded by the experienced and capable Eastern Front General Hasso von Manteuffel, a former CO of the *Großdeutschland* Division. This compromised the Panzer Lehr, 2nd and 116th Panzer Divisions, plus the 18th, 26th, 62nd and 506th Volksgrenadier Divisions. Finally, to establish a firm shoulder on the left flank of the operation and protect it from interference from Patton's US Third Army to the south, was General Erich Brandenberger's Seventh Army consisting of the 5th Parachute and 212th, 276th and 352nd Volksgrenadier Divisions. (The comparative weakness of Brandenberger's force was to be a major contributory factor in the eventual failure of the operation.) Again, it is significant that Hitler entrusted prime responsibility for the success of the plan to the Waffen-SS and his trusted old companion 'Sepp' Dietrich. He also had faith in Otto Skorzeny, who was in charge of a nominal brigade (the 150th) of volunteers dressed in American uniforms and driving American tanks, half-tracks and Jeeps, whose purposes were to sow confusion and capture petrol dumps; all of Skorzeny's men knew that if they were captured they would be shot as spies — as, indeed, many of

SS troops with captured American GIs during the Ardennes offensive. The man in the centre carries a Panzerfaust, *a German anti-tank weapon equivalent to the Allied bazooka.*

them were for the Americans learned of the deception from a prisoner on the first day of the battle.

The German force, over 200,000 men strong, with some 1,200 tanks and assault guns, was immediately opposed by approximately 80,000 American troops, many of them newly arrived in Europe and completely inexperienced, others from divisions which had been assigned to a 'quiet' sector of the front after being mauled in earlier battles. They were shortly to be rudely awakened — literally.

The German onslaught was preceded at 05:30 on 16 December by an artillery bombardment which shook the startled GIs out of their sleeping bags and into their snow-lined foxholes, then the tanks clattered forward under the artificial moonlight created by shining searchlights at the base of the clouds. From the German point of view the weather was ideal, for the low cloud ceiling would prevent the dreaded 'Jabos' — Allied fighter-bombers — from operating.

To begin with things seemed to be going well, although a parachute drop north of Malmédy was a disaster. A battlegroup of the Leibstandarte commanded by Obersturmbannführer Joachim Peiper broke through the Losheim Gap between the US V and VIII Corps and was soon heading rapidly for the Meuse, but the following columns became bogged down in monstrous traffic jams. Similarly, the 12th and 277th Volksgrenadier Divisions encountered much stiffer resistance from the American 2nd and

9th Divisions than had been expected and were unable to clear a path for *Hitler Jugend* on the right flank. To their south, Manteuffel's Fifth Panzer Army also made good initial progress, but was unable to capture the all-important road junction at Bastogne, defended by the US 101st Airborne Division which had been rushed to the spot despite the fact it was supposed to be resting after the heavy fighting in Holland. Similarly, the 82nd Airborne Division put up a stiff resistance at St Vith until pushed out on 21 December by the combined might of *Das Reich* and *Hohenstaufen*. But these limited successes were all that was achieved. The Army's 2nd Panzer Division got the furthest, reaching Celle, a stone's throw from the Meuse, but no units actually got across the river.

Recovering from their initial panic, the Allies responded strongly to the threat. General George S. Patton, who had been preparing his Third Army for a renewed assault in the Metz sector, wheeled his entire force through 90° and smashed his way through Brandenberger's Seventh Army to relieve the encircled airborne troops in Bastogne. By Boxing Day it was apparent to everyone that the offensive had failed and the Germans were retiring at all points, harassed by Allied fighters and bombers now the skies had cleared, and having to abandon much of their heavy equipment through lack of fuel. All the offensive had done was delay the inevitable end for a few weeks.

One unsavoury and still controversial incident must be mentioned. During their advance towards Malmédy on 17 December, one of Peiper's two columns overran a small group of stragglers from the US 285th Field Artillery Observation Battalion, 7th Armored Division, who were retreating towards St Vith. The sole American officer to survive what followed, 1st Lieutenant Virgil T. Lary, gave the following testimony at Nürnberg.

'It was decided that it would be best to surrender to this overwhelming force, the First *Adolf Hitler* Panzer Division as we learned later. This we did… We were all placed in this field, approximately 150 to 160, maybe 175 men… The Germans then, at the particular time, were continuing to advance in a southerly direction towards Bastogne[?], and one of their self-propelled 88 mm guns was ordered to stop, and it was backed around facing the group of personnel as they were standing in the field. After what happened, I have no doubt today that if they had been able to depress the muzzle of this gun into our group, they would have fired at point-blank range with their artillery into that group of men. [This has always seemed improbable to me. *Author*] They were not able to do that, however, because we were more or less in a depression below the gun and they couldn't lower it. So this particular self-propelled weapon was blocking their advance and it was ordered off. At that time they drove up two half-tracks and parked them facing the group, at a fifteen or twenty foot interval between the two. A man stood up in this vehicle, who I later identified at Dachau [Oberschütze Georg Fleps], and fired a pistol… into the group. At the time we ordered our men to stand fast because we knew if they made a break that they would have a right then to cut loose on us with their machine-guns.

'His first shot killed my driver. The second shot that he fired into the group then set off a group of machine-guns firing into this helpless group of unarmed American prisoners-of-war. Those of us who were not killed immediately in the initial burst fell to the ground… We continued to lay on the ground and the fire continued to come into us… When they ceased firing after approximately five minutes, maybe three minutes, they came into the group to those men who were still alive, and of course writhing in agony, and they shot them in the head… During the initial firing I was only hit one time.'

Later, as dusk fell, Lary dragged himself across a fence and hid under a pile of logs in a woodshed. The next day he managed to reach the American lines where his story was received with incredulous disbelief. There were another 19 lucky survivors.

Now, no one can deny that a massacre did take place, but there are discrepancies which have never been satisfactorily resolved. When the advancing Americans later arrived on the scene they discovered 71 bodies

Joachim Peiper seen here examining a strip of photographs during the earlier German Blitzkrieg through the Ardennes in 1940.

lying in the field, far fewer than 175 or even 150, and this lends credence to Georg Fleps's own testimony, in which he stated that he had opened fire because some of the prisoners made a break for the woods. Regardless, it was still an appalling deed. At Nürnberg the unit's commander, Joachim Peiper, was sentenced to death by hanging because, even though he had not been on the scene, the ultimate responsibility under military law was his. Fleps was executed but Peiper's sentence was later commuted and he was released from prison on parole in 1956, later settling under an assumed name in the town of Traves in south-east France.

In 1975 a former Maquisard, by that time a shopkeeper in the neighbouring town of Vesoul, recognized him and passed the news on to a journalist, Pierre Durand. After extensive investigation, Durand confirmed Peiper's identity and published the story in *L'Humanité*, a left-wing newspaper. Peiper began to receive anonymous threats and his neighbours shunned him. Finally, he received a warning to leave France by 14 July (Bastille Day), or he would be killed. Whatever his faults, Peiper was no coward, but he did take the precaution of sending his wife and teenage daughter away to safety. During the night of 14/15 July neighbours reported the sound of shots, but by the time the Gendarmerie arrived on the scene Peiper was dead and his house a blazing ruin. He had obviously attempted to defend himself because both a rifle and a pistol lying beside his body had been fired. His killer or killers have never been identified — but one wonders how hard the French police tried.

*   *   *

Just as we began this final section in the saga of the Waffen-SS at war with events in Hungary, so we must approach the end.

The situation at the close of 1944 was broadly as follows. In the north, on the Baltic Front, General Ferdinand Schörner had assumed command on 23 July, three days after the attempt on Hitler's life. He exchanged places in Romania with General Johannes Friessner who had the bad luck to be in command when the Red Army attacked in strength on 20 August, precipitating the overthrow of Marshal Antonescu and Romania's defection to the Allies. Schörner had approximately 30 divisions under his command, including the 11th and 23rd SS-Freiwilligen Panzergrenadier Divisionen *Nordland* and *Nederland*, the 15th and 19th Waffen Grenadier Divisionen der SS (lettische Nr 1 and nr 2) and the 20th Waffen Grenadier Division der SS (estnische Nr 1). Faced with overwhelming odds of some 80 Russian divisions (130 by mid-August), Schörner conducted a skilful retreat but was forbidden by Hitler to evacuate Estonia until mid-September, and only then because any other course of action would have resulted in the total loss of Army Group North (especially after Finland made peace). Even at this point, the new line from Riga to Memel would have caved in if *Nordland* had not made a forced march of 250 miles in four days to seal a breach. In the end, though, Riga had to be forfeited and Memel was besieged, leaving what was left of Army Group North in Kurland. Large numbers of men were evacuated by sea back into East Prussia, but the remainder fought on in this bleak Lithuanian coastal pocket until the end of the war, by which time there were only 200,000 survivors.

On 17 January 1945 Hitler recalled Schörner from Kurland to take over command of Army Group A — the former Army Group North Ukraine which would shortly be renamed again as Army Group Centre — in Poland. To his north, Himmler himself, a man of no military training or experience, had been given command of Army Group Vistula, tasked with the defence of Prussia and Berlin! If it had not been so tragic, it would have been comic. On Schörner's right flank, General Otto Wöhler had replaced Freissner as CO of Army Group South (formerly South Ukraine) in Hungary while Field Marshal Maximilian von Weichs's Army Groups E and F had conducted a steady retreat up through Greece and Yugoslavia, harassed by Tito's partisans and pressed by British forces which had landed in Greece at the beginning of October. Most of his troops would soon join the fighting in Hungary apart from *Prinz Eugen* which remained behind in Yugoslavia to the end of the war. Hungary was Germany's last bastion on

Tiger II of sPzAbt 503, now given the honour title Feldherrnhalle, *in Budapest during the closing days of the war.*

the Eastern Front and Hitler fought against its loss with suicidal fanaticism, declaring that the fall of Budapest would negate all the 'success' of the Ardennes offensive.

The principal German strength in Hungary was Obergruppenführer Karl Pfeffer-Wildenbruch's IV SS Panzer Korps (*Totenkopf* and *Wiking*) plus *Handschar* and *Horst Wessel*; *Florian Geyer* and *Maria Theresia* were trapped in Budapest itself, the Russians having completed their encirclement of the city on 26 December 1944. Throughout January *Totenkopf* and *Wiking* tried to break through to the city but were too weak after months of continuous fighting to penetrate the Russian lines to any significant degree. The 34,000 German and Hungarian troops in the Budapest pocket were squeezed into a rapidly shrinking perimeter and when IV SS Panzer Korps finally abandoned its relief attempts in early February, their only remaining choice seemed to be to try to break out. Unknown to them, for Hitler had insisted on a total security blanket, help was on the way in the shape of Dietrich's Sixth SS Panzer Army which had been withdrawn from the Ardennes and was heading for Vienna — over the protests of Guderian who had wanted it sent to Poland to reinforce Army Group Centre which was in equally desperate plight. But the Führer had a fixation about Budapest, so it was to Hungary that the finest surviving Waffen-SS formations were sent. The 16th SS Panzergrenadier Division *Reichsführer-SS* was also summoned from Italy, where it had been operating since May 1944, and thrown into the Hungarian maelstrom.

The troops trapped in Budapest attempted to break out on the night of 11 February; of approximately 30,000, only 700 managed to reach the German lines to the west, the remainder being killed or captured. The few survivors from *Florian Geyer* and *Maria Theresia* formed the rump of the new so-called 37th SS-Freiwilligen Kavallerie 'Division' *Lützow*. Budapest was a lost cause, but still Hitler persisted and in a mad operation codenamed *Frühlingserwachen* ('Spring Awakening') threw away hundreds of lives. The plan was for IV SS Panzer Korps and the Hungarian Third Army to hold the line west of Budapest while the Sixth SS Panzer Army thrust through between their southern flank and the northern shore of Lake Balaton, spilling out northwards up the Danube to Budapest and southwards down the line of the Sárviz Canal while Weichs's Army Group E laid on a diversionary attack north from the Yugoslav border to draw off the Soviet reserves. Looking at the maps in the Reich Chancellery, Hitler thought that this way he could not only recapture the city but also encircle Marshal Tolbukhin's 3rd Ukrainian Front in southern Hungary!

To begin with a preliminary manoeuvre was necessary to eliminate the bridgehead the Russians had established over the River Hron, a tributary of the Danube north of Budapest. The attack which began on 17 February took the Russians as completely by surprise as the Americans had been two months earlier in the Ardennes, for they not only themselves failed to detect Sixth SS Panzer Army's redeployment, but apparently ignored warnings from British intelligence via 'Ultra'. Thus they had no armoured formations on this sector of the front, and to begin with the Panzers went through their infantry like the proverbial knife through butter. By 25 February the German northern flank seemed secure enough to permit the second phase of the attack south of Budapest around the top of Lake Balaton, but by this time the Russians *had* woken up to what was happening and were prepared.

The assault was launched on 6 March under the worst possible conditions, for the start of the spring thaw had turned the ground to the usual gluey mud while snow flurries obscured vision. These obstacles so hampered II SS Panzer Korps's approach march that only I Korps of Sixth SS Panzer Army was in the right place for the beginning of the attack. Tolbukhin reacted with vigour, throwing everything available into containing the offensive, including Sixth Guards Tank Army. I SS Panzer Korps managed to advance 25 miles, II Korps only five. Then the Russian Marshal counter-attacked from the north on 16 March, threatening to cut off Dietrich's divisions. He was held by IV SS Panzer Korps only because fog and snow prevented the Soviet air force lending a hand, but the Third Hungarian Army was torn to shreds. Sixth SS Panzer Army was rapidly pulled back to hold the gap, but it was obvious that, as in the Ardennes, the over-ambitious plan had gone disastrously wrong. A full-scale withdrawal into Austria followed.

Nothing could now save Hitler's 'Thousand Year Reich', not even the Waffen-SS. Hitler, in Heinz Guderian's words, 'flew into a towering rage' when he heard that they were retreating out of Hungary. It was not the first time Guderian had experienced the Führer's wrath when the subject of the SS came up. On 13 February he had delicately but openly challenged Himmler's fitness to lead Army Group Vistula and had won a small victory after a heated two-hour verbal battle when Hitler finally agreed not just to appoint General Walter Wenck to the Reichsführer's staff, but to put him in tactical command. Now it was his long-faithful and long-suffering comrade 'Sepp' Dietrich's turn to feel the mad dictator's anger. In Himmler's presence, Hitler told Guderian to fly to Hungary and order Dietrich and the men of the Leibstandarte and his other SS divisions to tear off their armbands. (These, sewn in white or silver thread on black cloth strips just above the left cuff, were a proud identifying feature of each division or regiment within the Waffen-SS.) Guderian demurred, pointed out that such a task was really Himmler's province, but the Reichsführer himself was too cowardly to face Dietrich personally and had the order transmitted instead.

As it happened, many SS soldiers were already stripping their uniforms of identifying insignia to avoid the persecution they knew they would suffer when taken prisoner, but Dietrich took the order as a personal affront when it finally arrived. After calling his divisional commanders together in Vienna — the Leibstandarte's Brigadeführer Otto Kumm, *Das Reich's* Standartenführer Karl Kreutz (standing in for Oberführer Heinz Lammerding, who had been assigned to help Himmler out), *Totenkopf's*

In happier days — 'Sepp' Dietrich awarding a medal to one of his men.

Brigadeführer Hellmuth Becker and *Hohenstaufen's* Brigadeführer Sylvester Stadler* — he ordered them to refuse to pass the order on to their men. 'That's your reward for all you've done these past five years,' he is reported to have said. There is even an apocryphal story which is unfortunately most unlikely to be true, for Dietrich's own medals still survive in a private collection, that he stripped them off and returned them to his Führer in a chamber pot or latrine bucket!

Operation *Frühlingserwachen* was the last major offensive conducted by the Waffen-SS. By the time it was over the western Allies were across the Rhine and on 1 April Walter Model's Army Group B had been encircled in the Ruhr, another 'pocket' from which there was no escape. After nearly three weeks' futile fighting, the Field Marshal disbanded his forces and a few days later, on 21 April, shot himself rather than face the disgrace of surrender. The remnants of the 6th SS-Gebirgs Division *Nord* were among the units which entered American captivity here.

The survivors of the other Waffen-SS divisions either chose to go down fighting — whether in Vienna or the bomb-torn rubble of Berlin is really immaterial — or to gather their last tatters of dignity and try to surrender

---

* At the time of writing, Kumm and Stadler are still alive. Kreutz's fate is unknown but he would be 90. Becker was executed for war crimes. Lammerding was implicated in the Oradour massacre but after serving a West German prison sentence could not be extradited to France (where he had been tried and convicted *in absentia*) for execution and died peacefully in 1971. 'Sepp' Dietrich received a 25-year prison sentence but was released after just over 10 and died a free man on 21 April 1966.

with honour. By April 1945 the SS divisions no longer existed. Their depleted ranks were filled with airmen who had no aeroplanes to fly, by sailors whose ships had all been sunk, by policemen whose 'beats' had been bombed flat and by workmen of all classes who were given a rudimentary uniform, a few minutes' training in how to load and fire a rifle and were then thrust into the front line. Training schools were emptied of 16-year-old volunteers who displayed suicidal courage and old folks' homes were denuded of barely mobile grandfathers whose First World War experiences made them cynical, wary and unlikely seekers after Knights Crosses, whose only loyalty was to the survival of themselves and their families.

'Sepp' Dietrich held his remaining troops together with remarkable discipline. Of the Leibstandarte *Adolf Hitler*, 1,500 men with 16 tanks surrendered themselves into American custody in the Steyr area; the *Führer Begleit Bataillon* or Führer Escort Battalion, Hitler's personal bodyguard selected from the division's personnel, died almost to a man in Berlin defending their leader's ashes after he committed suicide on 29 April alongside his wife of a few hours, Eva Braun. *Das Reich* held out in Vienna until 15 April but was then forced out; its *Der Führer* Regiment fought against the Slovak insurrection in Prague at the beginning of May and succeeded in helping many of the city's inhabitants to flee from the Russians towards the west. *Der Führer* surrendered on 8 May and on 9 May the *Deutschland* Regiment, cut off and out of ammunition, also marched into American captivity. *Totenkopf*, with fewer than 1,000 men and only six tanks, surrendered to the Americans near Linz on the same day but most of the division's officers and men were handed back to the Russians, in whose hands their fate is best not imagined.

Of the Germans and foreign volunteers in the fourth of the Waffen-SS's premier divisions, *Wiking*, the majority surrendered at Fürstenfeld but many men managed to evade capture, slip into civilian clothing and escape to join the French Foreign Legion, seeing extensive later service in Indo-China (Vietnam). *Hohenstaufen* survivors surrendered alongside the Leibstandarte at Steyr. *Frundsberg* was less 'lucky' and had to give itself up to the Russians at Schönau. The youngsters of the *Hitler Jugend*, reduced from a confident band of 21,300 to a mere 455 battle-weary survivors, also managed to retreat west and surrender to the Americans near Enns in Austria. *Reichsführer-SS* gave itself up to British and American forces at Klagenfurt and Radstadt. *Götz von Berlichingen* finally gave up after 11 months' solid fighting to US forces near Achensee on 7 May.

* * *

It would be ideal to be able to write *finis* at this point, but May 1945 did not see the end of the Waffen-SS nor of the SS as a whole. Many of its higher ranking personnel succeeded in escaping retribution and fled to other countries, particularly South America and Spain but also the United States, through the auspices of the *Odessa* network popularized in the

Frederick Forsyth novel *The Odessa File*. Otherwise known as *Die Spinne* ('The Spider'), this was — and almost certainly still is — a Nazi self-help organization for which Otto Skorzeny claimed most of the credit after his escape from jail in Darmstadt on 27 July 1948. It was largely run from Madrid with Franco's tacit approval using laundered millions of pounds Sterling from plundered Jewish bank accounts and sales of innumerable looted works of art. The organization's aims were to get known wanted war criminals to places of safety beyond normal legal reach; to provide funds for legal assistance for SS men brought to trial and subsequently to establish them in commerce or politics in post-war Germany and elsewhere; and to provide a 'social security' safety net for those of the lower ranks who had given earlier loyal service and fallen on subsequent hard times.

Today, most of the 'old' Nazis are either dead or senile. Heinrich Himmler himself proved his own ideals far distant from those he demanded of his followers. Replaced by Martin Bormann as 'national leader' in the final defence of the Third Reich, he toyed with the idea of striking a separate peace through the Swedish Red Cross representative, Count Bernadotte, but was dismissed from all posts when Hitler found out about the tentative discussions — which were fruitless in any case because the Allies had determined upon nothing less than unconditional surrender. Dressing himself in an ordinary Army private's uniform, Himmler ignominiously sought to escape the fate to which he had hastened so many others, but when captured by the British he bit into a cyanide capsule rather than face trial and inevitable execution.

A hard core of SS men who were still young at the beginning of the war survive, together with their children and intact ideals, and 'the Brotherhood' does all it can to cleanse the Waffen-SS record, not least through subsidizing books produced and marketed by sympathetic German editors and publishers. This is not a novelist's fiction, but fact. To make my own position clear, I have never been affiliated with any political party or group of any persuasion, right or left.

To sum up, the Waffen-SS was, as I said in my introduction, a unique military formation. Its aggressiveness and its methods have often been called into question, but with few exceptions those who fought against the premier divisions (as opposed to some of the later undeniable riff-raff) have never denied their fighting skill or effectiveness. And it is against this record that they must be judged, not against their political beliefs (which were far from being unanimously Nazi in any case), nor because they were connected with the concentration camps, nor because their in-the-field atrocities have been given what sometimes amounts to excessive publicity. As fighting soldiers their best men were an elite, knew they were an elite, and acted with the arrogance such a knowledge usually produces. What other war record could you expect?

Index

The following index is divided into four sections for convenient reference. Following the General index there are further sections on Military and paramilitary units, Personalities and Places.